Transformed in His Presence

The Need for Prayer in Counseling

By

Roger Peugh, M.Div.

and

Tammy Schultz, Ph.D.

with

Deb Nicholas

BMH Books

Winona Lake, Indiana

www.bmhbooks.com

Transformed in His Presence
The Need for Prayer in Counseling

Copyright ©2005 by Roger D. Peugh and Tammy Schultz

ISBN 10: 0-88469-300-7
ISBN 13: 978-0-88469-300-0
Printed in the United States of America

Published by **BMH Books**
BMH Books, P.O. Box 544, Winona Lake, IN 46590 USA
www.bmhbooks.com

Unless otherwise noted, Scripture references are taken from the Holy Bible, New International Version, Copyright ©1973, 1978, 1984 by International Bible Society. Used by permission of Zondervan. All rights reserved.

Scripture quotations marked (NLT) are taken from the Holy Bible, New Living Translation, copyright © 1996. Used by permission of Tyndale House Publishers, Inc., Wheaton, Illinois 60189. All rights reserved.

Interior Design: Jim Folsom
Cover Design: Terry Julien

Contents

Dedication

To my mom, Barbara Schultz (1932-1999)
Her life was marked by continual,
intimate conversations with God.
She was my shelter in the storm and a source of joy.
— *Tammy Schultz*

To praying people in my life
My precious wife, Nancy, my Mother, Laura Peugh
Gordon and Agnes Bracker, Tom Julien
and countless praying friends.

What God has done to grow hunger in my heart
for Him can certainly be traced,
in significant measure, to their prayers for me.
— **Roger Peugh**

Preface

Counselors, pastors, teachers, social workers, student development staff, lay helpers, volunteers are deluged daily with overwhelming human need. As the demand has increased, education programs have responded to meet this challenge. Most Christian caregivers have received beneficial training in skills, theories, and practices of counseling.

However, exceptional methodology alone doesn't change lives. It is our conviction that *so many of us are trying to do naturally what can be done only supernaturally*. God never intended for us to help people in our own strength. God designed us to ask, seek, and knock (Matthew 7:7-8) for every breath we take, and especially when we seek to help people when life is hard.

Each chapter exposes an account from Scripture to teach about topics relevant to caregivers: The essence of prayer, counseling, suffering, waiting, burnout, the need for supportive friends, and a vision for renewal. Each chapter contains accounts and insights drawn from over 50 years of combined experience with various cultures in pastoral and mental health settings.

We did not write this book as another "ought." Thoughtful caregivers are tired of simplistic advice that demands they just try harder. We wrote this for caregivers, new and veteran, who are desperate for a better way. It is not a how-to guide or a guilt trip: It is an invitation to Him.

We want to help caregivers move from self-sufficiency, overwork, burnout, and futility to God-reliance. *Transformed in His Presence* is a rallying cry for caregivers and the hurting and hurtful people we walk with to call upon Him, get to know Him, so we can become more like Him.

— **Tammy Schultz**
— **Roger D. Peugh**
   Winona Lake, Indiana
   September 2005

What We Were Made For
Why a Book on Prayer and Counseling?

... If there ever came an echo that did not die away but swelled into the sound itself—you would know it. Beyond all possibility of doubt you would say, "Here at last is the thing I was made for." – C. S. Lewis

Tammy's Story

I had been asleep for more than an hour when I was awakened by the jangling of the phone. It was Yvonne, my dear friend, who had been out driving. She sounded troubled. "Could I come over to chat for a bit?"

"Of course," I replied. A few minutes later as we sat in my living room, the phone rang again. I was surprised once more. For the second time that evening I thought, *Who would be calling me this late?*

My dad's familiar voice was on the line and he came quickly to the point, with words for which I was unprepared. "Mom died, Tammy."

"No, Dad, no," I sobbed, "I just talked with Mom." It was the evening of Mother's Day and before going to sleep I had called her.

She had told me that she was so looking forward to coming to visit me in Indiana. We exchanged the familiar words we had shared with one another so many times: "I love you."

My mom was my best friend and the person who has had the greatest spiritual impact in my life. Now my spiritual mentor had died. During that night of sorrow, Yvonne never left my side. Without my knowing, my dad had called her first and asked her to be with me when I received his call. I will never forget the gift of her steadfast presence that night.

When I arrived in Winnipeg the next morning, I went directly to my mom's small apartment. My overriding purpose was to find her Bible and her prayer journals. Mom was drawn to conversations with our God like a kitten to a patch of sunshine. Throughout the last 35 years of her life, she had suffered a debilitating illness. Her numerous hospitalizations and hardships drove her to a different ministry than she had ever envisioned. The illness forced her to give up speaking to women's groups and teaching first graders and brought her instead to a quieter ministry—a ministry vital in its quietness. She spent her days praying for people.

Beside her bed I found her Bible and a stack of 39-cent notebooks filled with her conversations with God. I held them tightly in my hands. She had told me that one day I could have her journals, and the time had come. I found a quiet place and began to read page after page. With tears streaming down my cheeks, I was filled with the ache of her death. At the same time, I had never felt so loved.

I discovered page after page filled with conversations with our heavenly Father about my brother and me. She was relentless in taking our burdens and joys before God. She spent hours every day lifting us up like Moses holding up his arms on behalf of the Israelites (Exodus 17). I knew Mom was a woman of prayer. Talking with God was inextricably woven into the fabric of her life. Often people would call and she would pray for them over the phone. When difficulties arose, Mom would stop everything and propose, "Let's pray." Still, I had not fully grasped the depth of her relationship with God until that day surrounded by her prayer journals. Storming the throne of grace on behalf of her children and others was her sacred sacrifice and her utmost joy. Her love saturated me.

The disappointments and hardships in this world always thrust us somewhere. They pressed my mom closer to Jesus. She was physically weak, but spiritually powerful because of her intimate relationship with her Father. During the days, weeks, and months of grief following her funeral, I contemplated the inheritance Mom had left. She had little money and had left few material heirlooms. Yet, the legacy from my Texan-born mom was worth more than all the oil in Texas. I became increasingly aware that I could no longer depend on her to pray for all the day-to-day events in my life. It was my turn.

The legacy passed on to me was to hunger for God, and to pray for others as she had prayed. Mom, whose lifestyle was mostly sedentary, ran swiftly toward the heart of God. And now I held her baton—in the guise of 39-cent prayer notebooks—and I was beckoned to quicken my pace in the race she had run so faithfully toward knowing, loving, and trusting God. Her life emboldened me to quicken my pace, to race on.

D. L. Moody observed, "Every work of God can be traced to a kneeling figure." I am who I am today because of my kneeling mom. As with any inheritance, we can use it well by sharing it with others, or we can hoard it, gripping it tightly in our fists. Presently, my deepest desire is to pass my heritage on to others—to invite my students, friends, family, and others to be kneeling figures. Beckoning others to crawl up onto the lap of God is what I was made for.

Roger's Story

It was the middle of a Saturday afternoon. My wife and I had just arrived at the church where I was a pastoral intern while studying in seminary. We were there early to make final preparations for a youth function that evening. Suddenly, the side door of the auditorium swung open and in burst Pastor Bracker, my mentor. He was exhausted and evidently distraught. Quickly he spilled his heart: a suicidal man (we'll call him Adam) had left home with a pistol. The pastor had carried Adam's child on his shoulders for hours as they combed the fields near his house to find him, calling till he was hoarse.

There in the sanctuary he fell to his knees and began to sob, crying out to God for Adam and his precious wife and children. As the pastor wept and pleaded with God, I remember thinking that I knew nothing of this kind of praying. In the 14 years of my walk with Christ, I had been to many prayer meetings and seen some dramatic answers to prayer. But that day, as a newly married man in his early twenties, I asked God to teach me to pray with this kind of passion and intensity. God's deliverance of Adam from his self-destructive intentions helped fuel this growing flame in my heart.

At every opportunity, in every conceivable setting, and at whatever time of day or night, Pastor Gordon Bracker prayed with me and others. "Let's pray about it right now!" was his signature suggestion. He probably preached great sermons on prayer during those three years when I was an intern, but I don't remember a single one. Rather, it was his prayer habits that started to become my own. He prayed at the beginning of counseling conversations and again at the end. He prayed with people over the phone and encouraged everyone in the church to do the same. A sticker he had affixed to the church telephones said, "Pray with them before you hang up!" He prayed with people in hallways, in doorways, in hospital rooms, and outdoors.

The Brackers' prayer lives were shaped by love for God, compassion for people, and lots of pain. In early June, just a few months before our internship began, their youngest son, Ben, was killed in a head-on collision. Their mourning was still intense as a few weeks later the Pastor's appendix burst and he nearly died. Mrs. Bracker kept vigil at his bedside, writing countless thank-you notes to those who had consoled them at Ben's death, not knowing whether her precious husband would survive.

As I look back, it is easy to see that the Lord was using this devoted couple to woo me closer and closer to Him, developing habits I wanted to keep and deepen. And would it surprise you to learn that we never had so much as a hint of tension between us during the entire three-year internship and in the years following?

In 1987, just hours before he was to undergo heart surgery, I leaned over Pastor Bracker's hospital bed to pray with him one last time. Tears of love and thankfulness flowed freely as we told one another how we loved each other and talked with our God together. He never awoke from the operation.

Another baton was passed. Mrs. Bracker gripped it and began a ministry of intercession that continues to this day. This woman in her 90s has prayed for my wife and me and countless other people daily for the last 18 years, and is still praying today as this chapter is being written.

As my mentor went to be with the Lord, it was my passion to keep pressing hard after the heart of God and, as Pastor Bracker had done with me, to nudge as many as I possibly could to come to God's banquet table.

What We Were Made For

Through the praying lives of these beloved mentors, and through the great pain that life inflicts, we are discovering what it means to pray. Through prayer, and through God's generous love for us, we have found a place in His banquet hall—plates with our nametags, a warm and safe place where we are welcome and loved. We were made to spend our lives here. And we were made to find others whom we miss, and whom God misses, who were issued invitations but have not yet come. Some think they are not welcome. Others are lost in the thick darkness and the driving rain. Still others on their way have fallen among the rocks, or have been attacked and hurt in the night. Some have misplaced their invitations and do not realize they are missed.

We have chosen to be the seekers, to carry lanterns and flashlights out into the dark places, into the thick woods and the lonely fields and the steepness of mountains, where the rain swallows up the light and all people are alone. We are caregivers—counselors, pastors, social workers, missionaries, teachers, resident assistants, parents, and friends. And we will go.

Beckoning others to crawl up into the lap of God. This is what we were made for. Nudging as many as possible to come to God's banquet table. This is what we were made for. We entered the counseling ministry to help people heal and to help them discover God. We wrote this book to call people to commune with God by praying.

At Grace College and Seminary, Roger has taught the class called Principles and Practice of Prayer for more than 10 years. Some staff members from the Master of Arts in Counseling program took Roger's class and began to pray with Tammy, who chairs the program. Soon after, Tammy invited Roger to address the counseling department's faculty, staff, students, and their spouses on the subject of prayer and counseling.

Roger eagerly accepted the invitation. In preparation for that cold January evening in Indiana, Roger perused many of his nearly 150 books on prayer looking for anything on the subject. Then he looked at counseling books. The results of his lengthy quest? One chapter. During the past few years, a handful of books and articles have surfaced, but a complete work addressing the subjects of prayer and counseling together has been noticeably missing. We wanted to fill that lack, and so, this project was born.

The fledgling project was fresh on his mind when Roger ran into a colleague at a local office supply store. Among the aisles of computer programs, Roger stopped to chat, and the prayer and counseling project emerged in the conversation. "Hmm, prayer and counseling," she said after a thoughtful pause. "Those two topics don't seem to fit together."

She spoke matter-of-factly. Hers was an accurate observation, not a condemnation. Prayer and counseling have long been viewed as two separate and unrelated issues.

Tammy also was reminded of the estrangement of prayer and the practice of counseling when a man on a church's search committee approached her with a question. The man's church was without a senior pastor, and the committee was considering the qualities desired in a new pastor. Tammy referenced Acts 6:4, which explains that the spiritual leader is to be a praying man and one who loves the Word of God. The man responded, "Hmm, I never thought of that. I will add prayer to the list." His response stopped Tammy short. This individual had never considered that the leader of the church should be a praying man! This profound disconnect is tragic.

Through these and other experiences, the Lord has compelled us to write about the remarriage of the divorced couple of prayer and counseling. We believe that God is grieved over the divide of what He designed to be inseparable. We trust that you, the reader, will soon sense what we passionately believe: that true healing ultimately results from an encounter with God; and that inviting people to substantive life change—to be transformed—must be accompanied by calling on Him.

Reflection

Describe someone in your life who is a praying man or woman. What has he or she taught you about prayer?

CHAPTER ONE

Transformed
in His Presence
What Is Needed in Counseling?

Those who have left the deepest impression on this sin-cursed earth have been men and women of prayer. – Dwight L. Moody

The end of prayer is to be snatched away to God. – Gregory Palamas (1296-1359)

Jesus, I Come: Roger's Story

The stars were out overhead when my wife Nancy and I left the hospital after a long day. Nancy's mother, LaVerna, was failing rapidly. We tenderly kissed her and went home. At 1:30 A.M. the phone rang beside our bed. It was the nurse, reporting that Nancy's mom was quite agitated, wanting to get out of bed and walk home. "I'll be there in a few minutes," I replied. I splashed on some aftershave, grabbed a hymnal and drove to the hospital. When I entered her room she was awake.

I sat beside LaVerna's bed, took her right hand, opened the hymnal, and started singing—all the verses of all the songs I knew. I wept as I sang many of the hymns. One song especially moved me:

> Out of my bondage, sorrow and night, Jesus, I come, Jesus, I come;
> Into Thy freedom, gladness and light, Jesus, I come to Thee.
> Out of my sickness into Thy health, Out of my want and into Thy wealth,
> Out of my sin and into Thyself, Jesus, I come to Thee.
>
> Out of the fear and dread of the tomb, Jesus, I come, Jesus, I come;
> Into the joy and light of Thy home, Jesus, I come to Thee.
> Out of the depths of ruin untold, into the peace of Thy sheltering fold,
> Ever Thy glorious face to behold,
> Jesus, I come to Thee. (Sleeper)[1]

This old hymn has often been sung at the conclusion of church services, as people came forward to give their lives to Jesus. That night was the first time I had ever sung the words to a dying person, and they came alive with new meaning. My mother-in-law would soon be seeing Jesus' glorious face. Very soon she would be sheltered in His loving arms. Because the words were actually addressed to Jesus, I realized I was helping my frail mother-in-law sing a prayer to Him!

In the midst of the singing, LaVerna tenderly placed her other hand over mine. After ninety minutes of singing to a now peaceful woman of God, I said, "Mother, would you like to sit up?"

"Sure," she replied. I gently propped her against my shoulder and tenderly held her. "My, you smell good!" she said. I smiled.

"Mother, your catheter bag is empty, which means your kidneys are not working." I wanted to talk with her about her near departure.

"I wonder why that is?" she said.

"I don't know, Mother, but it means you will be seeing Jesus real soon."

"Oh, that will be great!" she responded enthusiastically. And then she added, "Roger, you're the best son-in-law in the world." That sentence was one of the greatest treasures my mother-in-law ever gave me.

I sang another 45 minutes and then slipped home so Nancy could come to be with her mother. A few hours later, she went peacefully into her Lord's loving arms.

I learned valuable lessons that night. As a dying woman, my mother-in-law didn't want to be alone. The words and melodies of the old, cherished hymns directed her attention to the Lord she loved. She needed God that night, and in her rapidly failing condition she needed someone to help her into His presence. With that help, she became peaceful.

Those precious hours remain my most treasured memory of our 30-year relationship. It was being with her, loving her, and being loved back so tenderly. It was helping her experience God's peace as she turned her gaze to Him. She didn't have the strength to formulate sentences that night. Words didn't matter. God saw her heart and her love for Him, and He flooded her with His peace.

It's not every day that caregivers sit with people destined to die before the sun rises. But it is every day that caregivers sit with people at their point of crisis—in places of pain and of impending change. Reflecting on that momentous final night with LaVerna illuminated some truths for us about counseling and prayer. Hurting people need God in their debilitating illnesses, rapidly failing marriages, paralyzing grief, deteriorating addictive behaviors, and seething bitterness. They need someone to help them become aware that He is always present.

The Lord is close to the brokenhearted (Psalm 34:18). But the fact is, when hurting and hurtful people enter the offices of pastors or counselors, most often they have not fully grasped the truth that their greatest need is to meet God. Even a client marching into a secular mental health center carrying an antipathy toward God desperately needs His life-changing touch. Sometimes precious little can be said at the start to escort hurting people into the presence of God. Much depends upon the attitude of the distressed person and the context of the counseling setting. At other times, those we counsel are like LaVerna—hungry, desperate, waiting to be positioned to encounter Jesus.

Troubled folks haul all types of baggage through caregivers' doors. People face all kinds of pain: vanishing jobs, deteriorating relationships, haunting memories. Countless individuals come to caregivers whispering, "I've never told anyone this before," and then tell agonizing tales of trauma and heartache. They reveal personal injuries that no human being should ever have to endure. This world is full of trouble. The valley of the shadow of death is fraught with gorges and unforeseen dangers; it is harrowing to walk with distraught people through that darkness.

In This World You Will Have Trouble

In Job 14:1, a haggard Job proclaims, "Man born of woman is of few days and full of trouble." Recording artist Pam Thum echoes this thought in the lyrics of a song, "Life Is Hard (God Is Good)."[2] The lyrics burst the bubble of Pollyannaish thinking. Jesus Himself said, "In this world you will have trouble…" (John 16:33).

Pain and distress are inevitable. Yet trouble, sifted through God's hands, has a special mission. Redemptive trouble was designed to prod us to call on the One who can help us in the midst of it. In Scripture we read about a variety of people in a mess who responded by calling on God. Exodus 2:23: "The Israelites groaned in their slavery and cried out, and their cry for help because of their slavery went up to God." And when they called God, "God heard their groaning and He remembered His covenant with Abraham, with Isaac and with Jacob. So God looked on the Israelites and *was concerned about them*" (2:24-25, emphasis added).

In Luke 18:13 a man who perceived his own hideous sin called to the Lord, "God, have mercy on me, a sinner." Our Lord experienced trouble and called on God. "During the days of Jesus' life on earth, he offered up prayers and petitions with loud cries and tears to the one who could save Him from death, and he was heard because of his reverent submission" (Hebrews 5:7). God heard each of these calls; He is forever listening for the sound of our voice.

E. M. Bounds, the prophet of prayer, born nearly two centuries ago, explained,

> Trouble often drives men to God in prayer, while prayer is but the voice of men in trouble...Prayer often delivers one out of trouble and, more often, gives strength to bear trouble, ministers comfort in trouble, and begets patience in the midst of trouble. Wise is he in the day of trouble who knows his true source of strength and who fails not to pray.[3]

What Only God Can Do

Through Roger's experiences among German believers, while serving the Lord in Stuttgart, Germany, he learned that Psalm 50:15 is commonly referred to by Germans as God's phone number: "And call upon me in the day of trouble; I will deliver you, and you will honor me." This is a number to highlight in any phonebook! Calling God in difficult times is the most fitting course of action for people in need. Yet, sadly, in this world of cell phones and instant messaging, we have observed that scores of Christian caregivers sit with people enduring desperate circumstances and do not dial God. Dashing to His side or leading others to call on God has not been considered a priority or a necessity.

Before his death, writer and professor Lewis Smedes was asked to observe a prominent Christian graduate school of psychology in order to reflect on the integration of theological and psychological understanding. He observed, "What has struck me most these past three months is this: I don't think Christian psychology is really clear about what it is that only God can do, as opposed to what psychotherapy can do to bring about healing."[4]

We have missed the proverbial boat. Many Christian caregivers have forgotten, misplaced, or have never written down God's number. How did this happen? We know that the western church in general prays little. To verify this fact, contrast Sunday morning church attendance with the number of people at prayer gatherings. Few seminaries have courses on prayer. Too few Christian schools of counseling have modeled and taught that it is the caregiver's high privilege and responsibility to ask God for help.

In educating Christian caregivers, we place a high priority on correcting erroneous thinking and changing behaviors. We give students a thorough understanding of ethics and laws, diagnoses, and addictions—all good material, and vital in today's world. However, we believe that too often we have relied exclusively on our exceptional education and our thorough research, and we have left the God of heaven on the periphery of the healing process. We have been *trying to do naturally what can be done only supernaturally*. Or, in Christian settings, we give God lip-service and tack prayer onto the end of sessions, more often as a signal to troubled folks that the session is over, than as a genuine plea for help.

Doubtless, many people we help become less depressed, develop better boundaries, and become more assertive; but too often we do not encourage them to call upon God in troubling times. Efforts to lead people not just to know *about* Him, but really to *know* Him, are missing.

In Terry Wardle's book, *Healing Care, Healing Prayer*, he explains,

> The goal of faith is neither right thinking nor right behavior. The central focus of the Christian life is growing closer to Jesus Christ and being transformed into His likeness...Information serves to help a person progress toward His embrace, and as such is useful and important. But information is never the goal. Jesus is the goal, and movement toward Him is the standard of personal health and growth...When an individual concentrates on knowing Him, his life will change and come into alignment with what the Lord desires.[5]

Why do we call on God? One reason is for His help. Most importantly, we call on Him in order to get to know Him. Paul said that his life goal was to get to know God: "I consider everything a loss compared to the surpassing greatness of knowing Christ Jesus my Lord..." (Philippians 3:8). Getting to know God changes everything. We are buoyed up by getting close to Him. A. W. Tozer, who without any formal theological education became a pastor and theologian, was a leader wise beyond measure. He explained that the godly people in history spent the most important part of their lives getting to know God.

> Come near to the holy men and women of the past and you will soon feel the heat of their desire after God. They mourned for Him, they prayed and wrestled and sought for Him day and night, in season and out, and when they had found Him the finding was all the sweeter for the long seeking.[6]

When we stand at the dark crossroads with hurting people, we believe it is our primary purpose to help position them toward God. We have brought a light and the comfort of our presence to where they were huddled alone; but we do not seek them in the valley of the shadow of death just so we can sit together in the dark. It is better to sit in the dark with a friend than to sit there alone; but to escort a friend out of the valley of the shadow and into the warmth of a welcome where they are expected—that is our mission. We go to guide people to a destination, to help them be aware of the One who is waiting for them.

If Roger had gone to the hospital that heartrending night just to talk with his mother-in-law, she might have been calmer than when she was alone; but she would not have had the peace of being led to the Father who was waiting to welcome her. Hurting people need more than us; they need the God of Heaven.

So That You May Believe

Mary and Martha of Bethany didn't hesitate to call God for help in the story recorded in John 11. Lazarus, their brother, was dying. They knew if they could just get him and Jesus together, their painful story would have a sweet ending. They sent a message to Jesus: "Lord, the one you love is sick" (v. 3), hoping He would come quickly to Bethany before it was too late.

Jesus, the healer and their good friend, had cured countless others of debilitating and terminal diseases. They believed He could and would heal Lazarus if He could just get there in time. He was their only hope. And He told the disciples reassuringly, "This sickness will not end in death" (v. 4). But instead of coming right away, incomprehensibly, Jesus "stayed where he was two more days" (v. 6). The delay was fatal. Lazarus died, and Mary and Martha were deeply disappointed.

Many of us can understand their despair, as we also have prayed and seemed to receive no answer. Perhaps that's one reason few Christians pray, or pray so rarely. "I asked God for help and it didn't do any good. My brother died anyway." Perhaps they pray again and the change in circumstances doesn't come. They become disillusioned and give up. We can all recall times when God could have changed things, but He didn't. And we don't understand.

What Jesus did next may offer a clue into God's ways. Jesus planned to demonstrate great truths about God to His disciples so they would know Him better: "For your sake I am glad I was not there, so that you may believe. But let us go to him" (v. 15). Our Lord let the circumstances deteriorate apparently beyond the point of repair. Why? So that his friends could learn how great He is, and could come to trust Him as never before. That is what He wants from all of us—for us to call upon Him for help, to nestle by His strong side, and to believe that He will do what is right, when it is right.

Often, in our work as caregivers, we see opportunities for healing come and go, and we wonder why God doesn't step in. We pray for a troubled marriage, but the spouse leaves with her lover. A child is abused again and again, and by the time she comes to us she seems pulverized, broken beyond repair. A son we prayed would leave his risky lifestyle calls and says he has contracted AIDS. We mourn, thinking that if only the healing had come in time, everything would have turned out well; but now it is too late—too late to heal, too late to do anything but bury our dead.

Overcome with grief and confusion from Jesus' *late* arrival and her brother's death, Martha came to meet Jesus on the road. "'Lord,' Martha said to Jesus, 'if you had been here, my brother would not have died. But,' she said, displaying a last desperate trust, 'I know that even now God will give you whatever you ask'" (v. 22).

At her time of greatest need, when all seemed lost, Jesus compassionately sketched a bigger picture of Himself. He said to her, "I am the resurrection and the life. He who believes in me will live, even though he dies; and whoever lives and believes in me will never die. *Do you believe this?*" (vv. 25-26, emphasis added). His penetrating question to Martha pierces us as well. Do we really believe Christ is the answer to life? Do we believe He is the answer to death, and pain, and all the suffering that comes through our doors?

As Jesus approached the grave of Lazarus, Martha warned that removing the stone that sealed it would discharge a putrefying stench. The body had been rotting four days in the Middle Eastern heat. Despite her faith and her assertion that "even now God will give you whatever you ask" (v. 22), Jesus' plan was too big for Martha to comprehend.

"Then Jesus said, 'Did I not tell you that if you believed, you would see the glory of God?'" (v. 40). What Martha already believed about Jesus would enable her to see that what He was about to do was a gift from God Himself. "When he had said this, Jesus called in a loud voice, 'Lazarus, come out!' The dead man came out…" (vv. 43-44). Death and despair were cast aside as heedlessly as the grave clothes wrapped on Lazarus' hands and feet!

Jesus' healing was beyond anything Mary and Martha had hoped for or imagined. They knew Him as a healer, and believed—with great faith—that He could save Lazarus from a terminal illness. But they never imagined He could raise a man from the dead. They never dreamed He could redeem a situation that was so far gone. And after Lazarus had his grave clothes removed, many believers saw the miracle and trusted Jesus (vv. 45-53).

Through the experience of Lazarus, Jesus wanted to bring His friends to a deeper level of relationship with Him. He wanted them to call out to Him for help, to trust Him, to look to Him and draw close to Him, to love Him. Mary, Martha, and Lazarus were forever bonded to Jesus with unshakable trust and deepest love. Every Christ-forgiven and Christ-transformed addict, murderer, thief, liar, adulterer, and pervert is eternally grateful, forever bonded to Him. They have received not just the unlikely, but the impossible.

We want to be like Mary and Martha and call on God when trouble comes. We want to trust Him long past the time when all seems lost. We want to see Him do things we cannot imagine. This book is a rallying cry to caregivers to call upon the Lord. It is an encouragement to us who help, to gather teams of people to pray for us as we sit with broken people. It is an invitation for caregivers of all kinds to lead fellow travelers on the pilgrimage to seek the Lord, to spend time with Him, to know Him, and to become like Him. To find true healing and joy, we must go to the source of all healing and joy—which is not ourselves, nor our compassion, our empathy, or our wisdom. It is the God of Heaven.

In our pursuit of the God of Heaven throughout the next chapters, we will look at several topics essential to our work as prayerful caregivers:

- **The nature of prayer**, by looking at the life of Mephibosheth in 2 Samuel 9.

- **The nature of Christian counseling**, using the account of four stretcher-bearers in Mark 1.

- **The problem of suffering**, by exploring why Joseph used the silver cup in Genesis 43 and 44.

- **The problem of waiting**, as the prophet Habakkuk had to learn to do.

- **The need for prayer support for counselors**, focusing on Moses, Aaron, and Hur in Exodus 17.

- **The challenge of working with people who do not believe as we do,** looking at the ministry of John the Baptist in John 3.

- **The nature of healing and transformation**, as illustrated in the life of the Apostle Paul in the book of Acts.

- **The problem of burnout**, as experienced by Elijah in 1 Kings 18 and 19, and by Moses in Exodus 18.

- **What it looks like to be a praying caregiver**, observing Nehemiah and some of the great men and women of prayer.

We will also be sharing life-stories gleaned from our combined experiences with folks from various cultures in pastoral and mental health settings. Be assured, examples of clients and parishioners are composites of real-life situations to protect confidentiality.

To Seek and to Save What Was Lost

Throughout this journey together, we pray that we communicate this fact clearly: we are not suggesting a simplistic three-step method, followed by prayer with people according to a certain formula, so that heavy burdens will suddenly disappear. Oswald Chambers wisely explained that we must not "deal with the human soul and with the ailments and difficulties of the human soul according to any (one) principle whatever. As soon as we get attached to a shortcut in dealing with souls, God leaves us alone."[7]

It is our prayer that the reader will understand we did not write this book as another *ought*. We are not suggesting prayer as yet another to-do item, a further rule to keep, a way to demonstrate that we are biblical caregivers. We have not written to add weight to anyone's already heavy load. We do not want to shame caregivers into praying more. Thoughtful people are tired of simplistic advice that merely demands they try harder.

What then can we do, if just trying harder does not work? If we are not burdening Christian caregivers with another *ought*, what is our call? We are offering what Jesus offered in Luke 19:1-10 when He spotted Zacchaeus sitting in the sycamore tree. Jesus told Zacchaeus—widely known as a swindler—that He wanted to be a guest in his home that day. And what was the response of the diminutive Jewish man? "Zacchaeus quickly climbed down and took Jesus to his house in great excitement and joy" (Luke 19:6 NLT). Jesus' words to him that day were not an accusation, but an invitation! Jesus did not "guilt-trip" this thieving tax-collector down out of the tree. He announced that He wanted to spend time with Zacchaeus.

We want the reader to experience the friendship and acceptance Zacchaeus enjoyed when he welcomed Jesus into his home that day. It was Jesus' invitation, not disapproval, that transformed Zacchaeus from a grasping, dishonest man into a man of integrity and generosity.

Christ's love is transformative. As we labor for transformation in the lives of caregivers and in the lives of the people we counsel—people whom we love, and God loves—our greatest goal is that we might know Him. We invite you to come with us on this journey—to meet with Jesus, and to beckon others into His presence. This is, beyond all possibility of doubt, what we were made for.

Reflections

1. Concerning the Lazarus story in John 11, Mary and Martha's first response to trouble was to call on Jesus. Where are you inclined to turn when you encounter difficulties?

2. God knows everything (Matthew 6:8). So why does He want us to call on Him when we are in trouble (Psalm 50:15)?

3. Lewis Smedes stated, "What has struck me most these past three months is this: I don't think Christian psychology is really clear about what it is that only God can do, as opposed to what psychotherapy can do to bring about healing."[8] What are your reactions to this statement and why?

Notes

[1] Sleeper, William. *The Hymnal for Worship and Celebration* (Waco, TX: Word Music), 1986.

[2] Thum, Pam. "Life Is Hard (God Is Good)," *Feel the Feeling* [CD] (Nashville: Benson Music Group), 1995.

[3] Bounds, E. M. *Prayer* (New Kensington, PA: Whitaker House), 1997, p. 312.

[4] Smedes, Lewis. "God and Prayer in Christian Counseling," *Christian Counseling Today*, 2003, 11, p. 10.

[5] Wardle, Terry. *Healing Care, Healing Prayer* (Orange, CA: New Leaf Books), 2001, p. 28.

[6] Tozer, A. W. *The Pursuit of God* (Camp Hill, PA: Christian Publications, Inc.), 1982, p. 15.

[7] Chambers, Oswald. (1993). *So Send I You: Workmen of God* (Grand Rapids: Discovery House Publishers), 1993, p. 160.

[8] Smedes, p. 10.

CHAPTER TWO

You Shall Always
Eat at My Table

What Is Prayer?

Prayer is keeping company with God. – Clement of Alexandria, an early
Father of the Church

*Prayer is talking to the Father, not simply because we are confused or
confounded, but because we are lonesome for Him.* – Judson Cornwall

...But Now I See

Eleven-year-old Tammy squinted at the blackboard, rubbed her
eyes, and squinted again. She fidgeted, stretched, and turned back to
the vague white lines on the black slate. Every day was the same until
the day eye examinations were provided at her elementary school.
Then she learned why all the letters seemed to swim and fade—she
needed glasses. A week later, Tammy and her dad walked hand-in-
hand out of the optometrist's office. Tammy proudly sported her new

glasses, and stopped abruptly when she reached the sidewalk. She gazed in awe at the trees across the street for several moments, then turned to her dad and exclaimed, "Dad, the trees have leaves!" The hazy green splotches she knew so well were now sharp and intricate with thousands of individual leaves.

Years ago, there was a man born blind. He had never seen the smile on his mother's olive-skinned face, or the sun sparkling off the water of the Jordan River, or the rich colors of a pomegranate, a fig, or a grape. Jesus met this man and directed him to put mud on his sightless eyes and to go wash in the Pool of Siloam. The man did as he was told—and for the first time in his life, he could see. Without delay, the religious men targeting Jesus interrogated the formerly blind man about his *supposed* healing. He replied, "One thing I do know. I was blind but now I see" (John 9: 25).

We all have *aha moments* from time to time, when something we were previously unable to see becomes clear to us. The reality of a matter, hazy and dim our whole lives, suddenly resolves into something distinct.

Like a healed man's first sight of the sun, like a small girl's first sight of individual leaves, Tammy reflects, "I am seeing prayer more clearly than ever before. Too often, I approached my time with my heavenly Father as an activity to be completed, rather than as a treasured friendship to be deepened. Prayer involves activity and discipline—giving time, perhaps writing down requests, going to a prayer gathering; but these important acts are not the core of prayer. I am beginning to see more vividly, more clearly: the essence of prayer is relationship."

Getting a grasp on the gist of prayer is not a simple task. Many people wiser than we have tried. Austin-Sparks astutely explained years ago that there is an element of mystery to prayer.

> I am very sure that when the last word of human
> experience about prayer has been said, we are still
> in the presence of the greatest of all mysteries. The

man who thinks he knows so much about prayer, that he can frame a philosophy of prayer, really confesses that he knows little indeed…With regard to this greatest of all subjects, there is really nothing further to be said than that which Paul said about all knowledge of God—"We know in part, and we prophesy in part."…What we know we know with a certainty which nothing can shake. But we only know in part.[1]

Much about prayer is still draped in mystery for us. But there is one thing we are learning about prayer, something we have come to know with a certainty—it is inseparably connected to relationship.

Seeing God in Others: Tammy's Stories

When I lived in Winnipeg, I spent Saturday evenings at my dear friend Kim's home. Kim and I would select gourmet meals during the week and then experiment on Kim's husband and kids. (Occasionally, zucchini was surreptitiously added into the entrée, and somehow the kids usually discovered these devious plans. Weeping, wailing, and gnashing of teeth would follow such occurrences!) After dinner, Tim would disappear to read while Kim, the kids, and I would pile into the car to rent a movie. On our return, bowls were filled to the brim with popcorn and smothered with butter and seasonings. Whoever made it to the couch first got first dibs. Ruby, the poodle, would hunt for the most comfortable lap, and the movie would begin.

I loved Saturdays. We laughed, spoke from our hearts, and created precious memories. In the end, it wasn't planning the lavish meals, watching good movies, or munching popcorn that made the evening. It was that my friend and I were together. I always felt I belonged. Kim's family made room for me at the dinner table and in their lives. Perhaps that is what our Heavenly Father designed prayer to be—dining with the best of all friends.

Not everyone has a friend like Kim. Many are lonely, bereft of close ties. Others have tasted relationships soured by betrayal, pain, and trauma. For some, involvements with others have become intimidating and even dangerous.

I worked with a woman who was in her twenties. It took months for her to whisper what she had never uttered before. When she was about eight years old, her uncle, a respected leader in the church, would look after her. It began with long walks, quarters, and handfuls of candy. But then came the trips to the shed. On a cold, damp bench, her uncle would lay her down and rob her tiny body and soul. As a little girl, she repeatedly prayed to God at night, "Please stop him." Then one day, during one of the trips to the shed, she mustered the courage to say out loud, "God, help me!" With a piercing gaze he responded, "God wants this." Years later, his evil words still cause me to shudder.

Sitting in my office long afterward, the woman still clutched the question that had never been answered: "Why didn't God stop my uncle? I begged God to stop him. But the abuse went on for years. Tammy, why didn't He stop it?" Behind this woman's question loomed a deep, dark well of mistrust for men and for her Heavenly Father. She cringed at the thought of being close to a God who would allow such a thing to happen.

Many who have endured abuse retain scars and walk with a limp. Countless others stand frozen, paralyzed, fearing the intimacy that would be part of getting to know God. It took many, many months—years—for this dear woman to begin to see that her Heavenly Father ached over the abuse her uncle perpetrated. It took time for her to release the lie that God didn't care, and to embrace the truth that God is good, even though people do evil things to little children.

This woman, who saw herself as dirty and damaged, needed even more time to realize that this good God longs to be near her—to grasp that this kind Father yearns to sit beside her at the royal table, not to harm her, but to adore her. From time to time, when she uttered her struggle with the question as to why her uncle violated her, do-gooders dispensed simplistic answers like quarters from a change machine. These clichéd words were like pouring lemon juice on an open wound. Eventually, however, she began to understand that God was anxiously waiting for her to reach the point of wanting to be with Him, too.

It is no surprise that the relationships we have with other people impact our intimacy with our heavenly Father. Many people are not lonesome for Him—they are terrified of Him. Such was the case for the guy with an unusual name.

You Will Always Eat at My Table

We come across this curiously-named man in the middle of the book of 2 Samuel, where a banquet is being held. A warm glow shimmers through the darkness. When we listen closely, we can hear laughter. Moving closer, we catch the aroma of food, rich and abundant. Sitting there is David, the great king of Israel, the man after God's own heart. His sons and daughters and friends lift wine glasses and talk and laugh. And beside the King is another man, with crutches propped against the table, like some ancient predecessor to Dickens' Tiny Tim. Someone calls him Mephibosheth, and fills his glass. 2 Samuel 9:13 explains, "And Mephibosheth lived in Jerusalem, because he always ate at the king's table, and he was crippled in both feet."

We step back in 2 Samuel to get the whole story of Mephibosheth, the last remnant of Saul's line. It begins in chapter 4, verse 4, with the briefest of notes: "Now Jonathan, Saul's son, had a son crippled in his feet. He was five years old when the report of Saul and Jonathan came from Jezreel, and his nurse took him up and fled. And it happened that in her hurry to flee, he fell and became lame. And his name was Mephibosheth."

A devastating battle took place at Jezreel; Saul and Jonathan were both killed, and Israel fell to the Philistines (1 Samuel 31:7). Under the pall of that defeat, little, unknowing Mephibosheth lost father, grandfather, and future. And as if losing high standing, wealth, honor, and influence were not enough, he was then robbed of his feet as well.

That is how we meet Mephibosheth, like some star-crossed character in a tragic novel. He fled to Lo Debar, a city in the nation now ruled by Saul's successor, David. In 2 Samuel 9:5 we read, "David sent and brought him from the house of Machir." Long, bitter years after Jezreel, when a grown Mephibosheth received a summons to the court of the king, we can only imagine what he must have thought. It has been a fairly regular custom throughout history for kings beginning new dynasties to kill off the previous king's family. Was this David's purpose? What else could it be? Mephibosheth had nothing to offer the king. He did not even live in a home of his own, but depended upon the charity of Machir. He was washed up, a cripple in an age that ostracized the disabled, without kin or any claim upon the world that had taken everything from him.

What dark and desperate thoughts haunted Mephibosheth on his journey to the king? Did he protest, "I never asked David for anything. I have done nothing to him. I have nothing for him. What does David want from me? Why can't he just leave me alone? I'm a dead dog dragging myself to the king to be kicked again."

When Mephibosheth hobbled into David's presence, "he bowed down to pay him honor." King David said his name, and he stammered, "Your servant!" The next words make us gasp, ringing out from the pages like gold coins falling onto gleaming tile. "Don't be afraid," said the King of Israel to the ruined man, "for I will surely show kindness to you for the sake of your father Jonathan, and will restore to you all the land that belonged to your grandfather Saul; and you will always eat at my table" (2 Samuel 9:6-7).

If you look closely at the passage, words that describe Mephibosheth eating at David's table are used four times (2 Samuel 9: 7, 10, 11, and 13). David certainly had no plans to harm this crippled man. Instead, he gave Mephibosheth all the land that King Saul had owned. What a magnanimous gift! And then the king elevated him to a seat of honor of which Mephibosheth never dreamed. He would eat "at David's table like one of the king's sons" (9:11). The invitation of David, the man after God's own heart, reflects and illustrates God's invitation to us. The King of all Kings bids us to join Him, through prayer, at His lavish banquet table.

Transformed in His Presence: Roger's Story

What occurs when we begin to spend time at the prayer banquet with the King? What happened to Saul of Tarsus after he called out to God on the road to Damascus (Acts 9)? What changes took place in Hannah when she poured out her soul to God in the temple (1 Samuel 1)? What impact on the life of Zacchaeus did his encounter with Jesus have (Luke 19)? What came to pass in each of these individuals when they moved into the presence of the King and called out to Him? All of them were transformed in His presence. They became more like Him.

When I was a young married student in seminary, my wife Nancy taught school nearby. I often stayed up late studying and writing papers. In the late afternoon I would prepare supper so that shortly after Nancy arrived home, we could eat together. But sometimes in the early afternoon I took a nap to dispel the weariness of the late night before. I didn't want Nancy to think I was being lazy while she worked, so I kept my nap a secret.

One afternoon as Nancy walked in from her day of teaching, she looked at me and asked, "Did you have a nice nap?"

Startled and a little embarrassed, I responded, "How did you know?" to which Nancy replied, "The pattern of the bedspread is all over your face!"

Where we have been will leave its mark upon us. As we spend time with the King, His desire is to transform us. What kind of change is He seeking? The kind of change where we look more like Jesus (Romans 8:29).

Who Is Transformed?

Old Testament believers were invited into God's presence or "into His courts with praise" (Psalm 100:4). This speaks of a specific place in the Tabernacle (and later the Temple) where God's people met Him. Since Christ died and the curtain of the Temple was ripped apart

(Matthew 27:51), all believers have the gift of direct access to Him all the time, through prayer. Henry Blackaby explained,

> In the Old Testament, the only access God's people had to the holy of holies, where God's presence dwelt...was through the high priest...We no longer have to go through an earthly high priest, nor do we have to make blood sacrifices anymore... We are no longer separated from the presence of God by a curtain because the veil has been torn in two.[2]

Now, prayer is how we meet God. It involves enjoying the King's presence; dining with Him, so to speak. But does everyone come to love Him when they sit across from Him at the royal feast? Is change in God's presence automatic?

What happened to Mephibosheth after he ate meals with the King? We find out in 2 Samuel 19. Mephibosheth's heart was tested when David's son Absalom betrayed his father. King David and his followers fled Jerusalem with most of David's household; but Mephibosheth stayed behind. Absalom "stole the hearts of the men of Israel" (15:6), and it appeared that despite David's kindness to him, Mephibosheth rejected him in favor of his son.

We learn, however, that far from deserting David, Mephibosheth was deceived by his servant Ziba and was left without transportation out of Jerusalem (19:26). Ziba told David that Mephibosheth was a traitor, choosing to stay in the city and serve Absalom. In reality, Mephibosheth remained loyal to the king. Distressed at David's departure, "Mephibosheth...had not taken care of his feet or trimmed his mustache or washed his clothes from the day the king left until the day he returned safely" (2 Samuel 19:24). He came to meet the king as soon as he returned to Jerusalem, overjoyed to see him again. Mephibosheth's heart was changed after spending time with King David at the banquet table, and he grew to love him and to remain loyal to him even when tested.

Do all who are invited to the banquet change, as Mephibosheth did—from fearing the king to loving him? Not necessarily. Many times we remain oblivious to God's presence, unaware that we share a table with Him. We are like two men insulting a co-worker, unaware that the subject of their ridicule is at the other end of the lunchroom table, hearing every word. They freely speak caustic, acrimonious words because they don't realize anyone is listening.

Remember the Pharisee who stood in the temple praying, "God, I thank you that I am not like all other men—robbers, evildoers, adulterers—or even like this tax collector. I fast twice a week and give a tenth of all I get" (Luke 18:11-12). Both the Pharisee and the tax collector were in God's presence, but one came with a humble and teachable spirit and the other came swollen with arrogance. One man prayed and left changed, and the other man prayed and left as arrogant as he arrived. Change in God's presence is not automatic. God addressed the people of Israel, who had kept their traditions but rejected Him in their hearts, with these chilling words: "When you spread out your hands in prayer, I will hide my eyes from you; even if you offer many prayers, I will not listen" (Isaiah 1:15).

Transformation involves an awareness that we are always in God's presence. This awareness can prompt us to talk with Him and realize that we are the tax collector in desperate need of forgiveness—that we are Mephibosheth, lost and lame. Real change involves coming before the King with a humble and grateful heart. The tax collector knew his need, and Mephibosheth knew what he had been given. "The sacrifices of God are a broken spirit; a broken and contrite heart, O God, you will not despise" (Psalm 51:17).

And We Are Happy

God does not give invitations to His table half-heartedly. He is eager for us to come—like a father yearning for his prodigal son to return home; like a man asking his true love to marry him. His invitations are costly. They were printed lovingly with the blood of

His Son. What could be the reason that the King of all Kings wants us to accept His invitation to the prayer banquet table? So we can become close with Him (Hebrews 10:22).

We are seeing "the leaves" more clearly than ever before—that the center of prayer is about coming near to God and allowing Him to shape us, to change us, to transform us, and simply to adore us. Prayer is simply and wisely summed up by an unknown, impoverished eighteenth-century peasant. When a pastor questioned him about what he did during the countless hours he spent sitting in church, the elderly man replied simply, "I look at Him. He looks at me. And we are happy" (as quoted in Syswerda).[3]

Reflections

1. Ponder your prayer life. Is it more like an activity or a relationship?

2. Crippled Mephibosheth referred to himself as a "dead dog" (2 Samuel 9:8) in King David's presence, wondering why the King should take note of him. Yet Mephibosheth was assured a daily place at the King's table because of David's kind invitation. When Christ-followers see themselves exclusively as "dead dogs," what effect does that have on their prayer lives?

3. What would happen if we regularly relaxed and spent time with our King at the banquet table rather than hurriedly shouting our orders at the drive-through window?

Notes

[1] Austin-Sparks, T. *Prayer: The Writings of T. Austin-Sparks*, Vol. VII (Jacksonville, FL: The SeedSowers), n. d., p. 95.

[2] Blackaby, Henry. *Worship: Believers Experiencing God* (Nashville, TN: LifeWay Press), 2004, p. 30.

[3] Syswerda, Jean E. *The Prayer Bible*. (Wheaton, IL: Tyndale House Publishers, Inc.), 2003.

CHAPTER THREE

Building Bridges and Digging Holes
What is Christian Counseling?

Talking to men for God is a great thing, but talking to God for men is greater still. – E. M. Bounds

...The Christian leader must be in the future what he has always had to be in the past: A man of prayer, a man who has to pray, and who has to pray always. – Henri Nouwen

We Keep Using This Word

"Incontheevable!" It comes bursting out almost of its own accord, this favorite line from a favorite movie—*The Princess Bride*.[1] The spoof on a swashbuckling romance boasts a huge following, most of whom can't sit quietly through it without blurting out their favorite lines along with the characters. Evil Vizzini and his not-so-evil crew capture the lovely Princess Buttercup, without fear of pursuit. Still, Inigo Montoya, the Spanish swordsman, keeps claiming the impossible. A masked man is following them. Vizzini brushes him off, lisping derisively, "Inconceivable!" to every insistence from Inigo.

But the masked man defies death and keeps coming, and as he scales the final obstacle, Vizzini peers at him in disbelief and screeches, "Inconceivable!" Inigo quietly turns to him and murmurs, "You keep using that word. I do not think it means what you think it means!"

In the face of much contradictory evidence, Vizzini still insisted that the masked man's pursuit of them was inconceivable. He made up other reasons that the man could be behind them, or flatly denied that the mystery man was there at all. Either he was deep in denial, or the word simply did not mean what he thought it meant.

Similarly, in the face of much contradictory evidence, many people use the term Christian counseling to describe their work with hurting individuals, when frequently, it doesn't look much different from secular counseling. Perhaps the term Christian counseling does not mean what we think it means.

Neil Anderson, in a presentation to the American Association of Christian Counselors, asked the question, "If someone watched your counseling sessions, would [the observer] know the difference between you and a non-Christian counselor?"

Sadly, the answer for many is no. Perhaps we do not know what it is we are aiming for. If Christian counseling does not mean what we think it does, what does it mean? What does it look like?

To Build a Bridge

People often change for the better with the help of both Christian and non-Christian caregivers. But we believe substantive life change is more than a rearrangement of circumstances, and it is more than a modification in thinking. We agree with Terry Wardle who said that Christian counseling must go further than decreasing cognitive distortions and changing behaviors. "There has to be something beyond helping people make changes in the way they think or act. I want them to experience a change that goes deeper, a change that can only come by the hand of God."[2]

McMinn expressed similar sentiments.

> If God longs to be in relationship with us and
> if the deepest longings of the human soul point to
> God, then the goals of Christian counseling go much
> deeper than changing behavior…These longings are
> spiritual in nature and so it is inevitable that every
> counseling session that digs beneath the behavioral
> veneer of human experience has something to do
> with spirituality and religious experience.[3]

We agree that God must be a part of real change. So what is it
all about, this profession, this ministry, this calling that we name
Christian counseling? What is the essence of helping hurting and
hurtful people through life's difficulties that is different from what
secular caregivers offer? Kellemen explained,

> Soul care…is coming alongside people to
> comfort them in their suffering. Spiritual direction
> refers to the role of confronting people about their
> sin and challenging them to grow in grace…We have
> a tendency to focus *either* on suffering or sinning. We
> see our counselee either as a victim to be comforted,
> or a sinner to be confronted. Biblical counseling
> is not either/or. It is *both/and…The counselor acts as a*
> *conduit. Counselors build bridges from the counselee to Christ and*
> *to other Christians* (emphasis added).[4]

Kellemen asserted that Christian caregivers are designed to act
as a bridge. But the most important question is—how does this take
place? Counseling does not become Christian simply because prayer
is offered at the beginning and end of every session. Using Christian
language or quoting Bible verses does not make it Christian. In fact,
using these practices immediately in a secular setting with a non-
Christian client would likely be unethical or worse, drive people away

from Jesus. A wise St. Francis of Assisi said, "Preach the Gospel to all the world, and if necessary, use words."

The point of Christian counseling involves leading people one step closer to Jesus so they can see for themselves that He is our Redeemer. And often this is done best with only a few words, or (when people are not yet ready to talk to God), through unuttered prayer.

To Dig a Hole

The older we become, the more we realize Jesus taught that the essence of life is loving God and loving others (Matthew 22:34-40). Caregiving, then, is helping others to love God and to love people. This is an uncomplicated concept, but it is not easy. Counseling is not easy. Facing staggeringly complex human entanglements, multiple losses, trauma, and addictions is anything but easy. But perhaps we have added to the burden by making the task more complex than our Lord intended. He knows that against the rigors and sorrows of a fallen world, we are only dust (Psalm 103:14). He intentionally fashioned us to need and enjoy interdependent relationships with each other and to live our lives dependent upon Him. God does not want His children to be alone, living in isolation from Him and others in self-absorbed self-sufficiency. He never wanted us to lend a hand to hurting people all by ourselves. He wants us to ask Him for help as we walk with broken individuals. He alone can meet people's deepest needs and longings; He alone can heal our agonized souls.

We find in Mark's Gospel an encounter between a man and Jesus that depicts the core of Christian counseling. Mark's first few chapters open with Jesus traveling in the northern region of Galilee where He became an immediate celebrity. One man was healed of the gruesome, incurable disease of leprosy (1:40ff). He excitedly shared everywhere he went what Christ had done for him. The amazement, wonder, and curiosity of the crowds meant that "Jesus could no longer enter a town openly but stayed outside in lonely places. Yet the people still came to him from everywhere" (v. 45). Mark then records an astounding encounter with a paralyzed man. If ever there was a man who was truly loved by his friends, we find him described in Mark 2:1-12.

> A few days later, when Jesus again entered Capernaum, the people heard that he had come home. So many gathered that there was no room left, not even outside the door, and he preached the word to them. Some men came, bringing to him a paralytic, carried by four of them. Since they could not get him to Jesus because of the crowd, they made an opening in the roof above Jesus and, after digging through it, lowered the mat the paralyzed man was lying on. When Jesus saw their faith, he said to the paralytic, "Son, your sins are forgiven." Now some teachers of the law were sitting there, thinking to themselves, "Why does this fellow talk like that? He's blaspheming! Who can forgive sins but God alone?" Immediately Jesus knew in his spirit that this was what they were thinking in their hearts, and he said to them, "Why are you thinking these things? Which is easier: to say to the paralytic, 'Your sins are forgiven,' or to say, 'Get up, take your mat and walk'? But that you may know that the Son of Man has authority on earth to forgive sins..." He said to the paralytic, "I tell you, get up, take your mat and go home." He got up, took his mat and walked out in full view of them all. This amazed everyone and they praised God, saying, "We have never seen anything like this!"

Jesus was teaching curiosity-hounds and blessing-seekers in a house packed as tightly as a Tokyo subway at rush hour. Four men arrived carrying their paralyzed friend to be healed by Him. Confronted by an impenetrable crowd, they sized up the situation and formulated

Plan B. Unable to get the man on the mat to Jesus through the crowd, they climbed to the spot directly above Him and began dismantling the roof! The text records no protest by the owner, no outcry from the crowd in the room below, no suggestion from Jesus or the swarm of people that they move outside to make it easier. These four tenacious men cared much about the healing of their disabled friend and little about the mess they made by creating a huge hole above Jesus. Straining, they lifted man and mat to the roof and gently lowered him directly into the presence of Jesus. Talk about loving friends!

TV cameramen today would have caught the astonishment on the faces of the crowd as the mat was lowered. A reporter would have exclaimed about this dramatic interruption of Jesus' sermon with a spectacle on the roof! Mark states simply, "Seeing their faith, Jesus said to the paralyzed man, 'Son, your sins are forgiven'" (2:5). All five men believed Christ could heal if only this encounter could take place. Jesus noted their simple trust in His ability to deal with the impossible circumstances this crippled man had endured for so long. God loves it when His people trust Him!

The disabled man was brought to Jesus, the only one who could free him of his paralysis, but he came away with more than just a healed body. Jesus can and often will change our circumstances, heal our bodies, prompt an adulterous spouse to give up the affair, rescue us from financial straits. But sometimes He does not. And when He does not alter our situation, He still, without exception, desires to ease our greatest struggle—our tendency to live independently and alone, alienated from Him.

The friends of the disabled man are remarkable examples of what Christian counselors are called to do. Christian soul care is all about helping people discover the *presence* of Jesus. The friends of the disabled man ripped the roof off to get to Jesus. What price will we pay to help hurting people find Jesus? This is the crux of true transformation, teaching others to "approach the throne of grace with confidence, so that we may receive mercy and find grace to help us in our time of need" (Hebrews 4:16).

To Be in the Presence of Jesus

Perhaps, like us, you wonder what could be meant by the phrase *into the presence of Jesus*. The stretcher bearers brought their disabled friend directly into the physical presence of our Lord. Today, when we guide someone into the presence of Christ, we can't do it physically.

Since God is omnipresent, every person on this earth is always in His presence (Psalm 139:7-12). However, though He surrounds us at all times, our sin ruptures our closeness with God. God told the nation of Israel, "But your iniquities have separated you from your God; your sins have hidden his face from you, so that he will not hear" (Isaiah 59:2).

The prophet Jeremiah gave a hope-filled message to sinful Israel as to how the closeness can be restored. "Then you will call upon me and come and pray to me, and I will listen to you. You will seek me and find me when you seek me with all your heart. I will be found by you" (Jeremiah 29:12-14). To enjoy the presence of God, or in other words, to enjoy being close to Him, we need to tell Him we are sorry for the ways we hurt Him and others. We must call Him. And we don't have to shout, because He is closer than our skin.

Discovering that God is with us all the time is like using a cell phone that is constantly connected (1 Thessalonians 5:17; 1 Chronicles 16:11). God is listening on the other end 24/7. In fact, prayer is far better than any cell phone since there are no batteries to go dead, we are never out of range, and the signal is never garbled, He never misses our call and He has prepaid all charges! And whatever language we speak, He speaks, also.

Roger reflects: Starting in my teen years, I have been fascinated with electronic devices and have learned a great deal. Recently, however, I was embarrassed by my ignorance. I had been accessing the Internet in my office using a dial-up connection, believing it would be quite complicated to hook up to the school's faster network. After two years of delay, I finally contacted the Computer Services Department and asked how much trouble it would be for them to help me connect to the Internet via the campus network. I told them I already had the appropriate cable. "All you have to do is plug in the cable," they told me. Sure enough! The moment I plugged in the cable, it worked. I was mortified. The high-speed Internet connection, less than three feet from my computer, had been available for at least 24 months but sat unused because of my lack of knowledge.

God is present with us always, closer than our breath, waiting for us to spend time with Him. Long before the first Christmas Eve, Isaiah prophesied (Isaiah 7:14) that God would send a child who would be called "Immanuel," which means "God with us" (Matthew 1:23). When the prophecy came to pass six hundred years later, Judean shepherds rushed to the Bethlehem manger to verify that God had truly taken up residence among us. Christians worldwide hear this truth in song each December as we celebrate Christmas. As we struggle to find words to explain what it means to be in the presence of God, we ask ourselves the question, "How would an adult explain this to a four-year-old?" We would say, "God is right here beside us like I am beside you. In fact, when you have asked Jesus into your heart, He is inside you."

True caregiving helps people come awake to the fact that God is with us. As C. S. Lewis said, "We may ignore, but we can nowhere evade, the presence of God. The world is crowded with Him. He walks everywhere incognito. And the incognito is not always hard to penetrate. The real labour is to remember, to attend. In fact, to come awake. Still more, to remain awake."[5]

The Lord Who Heals

We can't make people change. But we can encourage hurting people to spend time with the One who offers the best kind of change. When the disabled man on the mat was physically healed by Jesus, he was faced with a choice, the choice of how he would live the rest of his life. He could hang onto bitterness over all the years he had been unable to walk. He could refuse responsibility for the rest of his life, saying he had suffered enough and would now live for pleasure. But Jesus had also forgiven his sins—He had wiped away all the bitterness in his past and had given him a new start on life. If he had chosen the road of bitterness, his friends could have discussed old hurts, challenged his negative thinking patterns, and processed his relational style.

Ultimately, though, his friends could not change his heart. They could not heal him. But they did the greatest thing they could for him—they led him to Jehovah-Rophe, The Lord who Heals (Exodus 15:22-26, Jer. 30:17). And their friend rose and walked, and he no longer needed his mat or his old way of living. This is what true transformation is all about—leading people to the One who heals.

What We Think It Means

In the turmoil of working with tormented individuals, what does it look like lovingly to lower a hurting person through a rooftop—smack dab in front of Jesus? Phil shows us through his journey with a young girl we will call Melina.

A counselor in a residential facility, Phil began talking with Melina, a 16-year-old, articulate, well-mannered African American who lived in the facility for a time. She told her story with little emotion, as if reporting it on the evening news rather than sharing from her life. Melina, her sister, and her four brothers grew up in the projects in a Midwestern city. Her mother's crack cocaine addiction led to Melina and two younger siblings being removed from their home when she was about five years old. Over the next ten years, Melina went from one foster home to another with some occasional returns to her mother's care.

Initially, Melina did not understand why she had been removed from her mother. Then as she grew older, she realized her home was different. She recalled one night when her mother asked for her help in finding money lost in the front lawn. Together, they searched in the dark with a flashlight for money that Melina believes was not lost and probably did not even exist.

Melina's mother engaged in sex for drugs or drug money. Her six children were fathered by multiple men. Melina did not know her father. She said she still loved her mother. Although she said she did not hate her, she resented having to act as a parent when she was still a young child. She longed to recover the childhood stolen by her mother's addiction.

Melina relayed a vivid memory of sexual abuse by one of her mother's drug friends shortly before she was removed from the home. She wondered, out loud, whether or not her mother knew about the abuse and had covered for the attacker. She wanted to see the abuser shackled in prison, but believed that he had gone undetected and unpunished.

Phil asked about her ability to trust others, and Melina told him of her attraction to gangs. Gangs, she explained, provided her drugs (to escape her pain), fun (that she had missed out on as a child), protection (from her attacker that she did not have), provision (lacking at home), and a strong sense of security (which was an overarching theme in the conversation).

Melina had big dreams for her future—to finish high school and college, and then to become a family doctor. Thinking about the long and difficult road to such lofty goals, she sighed, "Sometimes I give up on myself."

Phil was overwhelmed. He realized that Melina's pain and many fears were far more than he could handle. At the same time, he was struck by the fact that for a brief window of time, Providence brought their lives together. "What could I do?" Phil asked, looking back on that time. "Where could I take her for help but into the presence of the best of all Fathers?" He asked God to help him be a representative of Him until she learned to trust Him on her own.

As Phil brought their first session to a close, he asked Melina if she would like him to pray for her. She admitted that she knew only a few Catholic prayers. Phil responded that a Protestant prayer would sound different because it wasn't memorized. Instead, he explained, he spoke to God as he would to a trusted friend. Curious, Melina consented. After he finished praying, with wide eyes and a big smile she exclaimed, "That was awesome!"

Much later, at the end of their last meeting, Phil asked Melina if there was anything he could do for her before she left. The road ahead seemed to be more difficult than she had anticipated. Her simple request warmed his soul.

"Would you please say one of those pro, pro ..." she tried, unable to remember the word Protestant. He helped her: "A Protestant prayer?"

"Yeah," she laughed with her eyes smiling.

Reflections

1. Describe your typical way of counseling others.

2. What is your answer to Neil Anderson's question, "If someone watched your counseling sessions, would [the observer] know the difference between you and a non-Christian counselor?"

3. Do you believe that the role of the four friends of the paralytic (Mark 2:1-12) is an apt picture of how caregivers ought to view their role in helping others to change? Why? Or why not?

4. We have proposed that helping people become aware of God's presence is a central facet of counseling. How is God awakening you to His presence? What would it mean for you to begin to awaken people to God's presence?

Notes

[1] Scheinman, A., & Reiner, R., Producers; Reiner, R., Director. *The Princess Bride* [Motion Picture] (Santa Monica: MGM Home Entertainment), 1987.

[2] Wardle, Terry. *Healing Care, Healing Prayer* (Orange, CA: New Leaf Books), 2001, p. 11.

[3] McMinn, M. "Exploring the Role of Religious Experience in Counseling." *Christian Counseling Today*, 6, 1988, 6-19.

[4] Kellemen, Robert W. *Soul Physicians: A Theology of Soul Care and Spiritual Direction* (Taneytown, MD: RPM Books), 2004, p. 25.

[5] Lewis, C. S. *Letters to Malcolm: Chiefly on Prayer* (New York, NY: Harvest/ HBJ Book), 1964, p. 75.

CHAPTER FOUR

The Gift We Really Need
Why Does God Allow Suffering?

Pain and prayer are partners. – Peter V. Deison

*It is weakness that keeps driving us, driving us to God by the overwhelming
conviction that we've got nowhere else to go. There is no help but Him. There
is no hope but Him.* – Joni Eareckson Tada

*Trouble makes earth undesirable and causes heaven to loom up large in the
horizon of hope. There is a world where trouble never comes. But the path of
tribulation leads to that world.* – E. M. Bounds

The Deep Waters

In 1997 theater-goers around the world flocked in record
numbers to see the summer blockbuster *Titanic*. The fictional love
story, woven into historical events, struck a deep chord within many
viewers. An observer in the theater seats those days would have seen
rows of usually self-possessed individuals gripping armrests or crying
unabashedly, both for the romantic characters, Jack and Rose, and

also for the movie's extras—all those nameless faces who perished in the cold, dark seas. Our hearts ached as the iceberg devastated the ship's mighty hull and the passengers milled about, still unaware of their peril. We knew what was going to happen. History recorded thousands of deaths, and we knew we were looking at doomed men and women. As the scenes advanced and panic grew, as crowds of people rushed the lifeboats, as the ship tilted and swung and passengers jumped or clung to the icy railings, the audience wept. We cried for their terror, for their selfishness as they turned on one other, for the doom that had fallen more than eighty years before in the frigid North Atlantic.

We would like to think that if we had been in their place, we would not have swamped a lifeboat or clutched another person and pulled him under the waves with us. We like to think we would have borne our last moments in courage and peace, praying to the Father we would soon see, or helping someone else hold on. But we know better. In the midst of that kind of terror we reach out to grasp something, anything—anything at all that will save us from the deep waters. Self-preservation is instinctive.

There are moments in our lives that feel like we are drowning. Many of you have felt it—the cold panic that races across your skin and strangles your heart; the desperate dread of some unavoidable catastrophe; the feeling of a physical weight that bears down upon your chest and makes it hard to breathe. We feel we are going under, never to resurface. David described it in Psalm 69:2 when he wrote, "I sink in the miry depths, where there is no foothold. I have come into the deep waters; the floods engulf me."

Suffering always drives us somewhere. It impels us to clutch at someone or something, anything available—a railing on a ship, pills, money, loved ones, Jesus. It is hard to sit still when we face catastrophe. People come to caregivers most often when they are in crisis. They are frantically looking for something to hang on to.

Katie-Mae, an ancient cat at 16 years of age, was losing weight. Her organs were beginning to fail, and she teetered slowly around the house on spindly legs. Katie-Mae was Tammy's faithful companion ever since she found her under her car, a scrawny kitten, almost frozen on a 40-degree-below-zero Winnipeg winter evening. Years later, her body failing, she would totter to wherever Tammy was sitting in the house and nestle as close to her as possible. The pain of a deteriorating body pressed this old cat to her owner's side. Tammy, who cared about Katie-Mae, wanted to bring comfort to her old friend. She desired to be near her as well.

In the best of cases, instead of pushing us to act self-destructively or to hurt those around us, pain can draw us close to God's side. Katie-Mae, a simple creature with none of humanity's alienating pride, instinctively drew near to the person who had been a source of comfort and provision in her life. But only because Katie-Mae knew and trusted Tammy did she turn to her in her hour of need.

We see this concept illustrated in the narrative of a man who knew sorrow like his own name.

A Brother Lost

The story begins in an era when many men had more than one wife. Jacob had four wives. Rachel was his favorite. She bore Jacob two sons, Joseph and Benjamin, Dad's favorite kids. Joseph's several stepbrothers seethed with jealousy and anger at their father's blatant favoritism. One day they snapped and took Joseph prisoner, selling him to slave traders traveling through Canaan and into Egypt. To hide their cruel deed, they let their father believe that Joseph had been killed by a wild animal.

Years later, the wife of Joseph's boss, furious over a failed attempt at seduction, lied about him and had him imprisoned. Yet, "the Lord was with him" (Genesis 39:21, 23).

Much later, through some amazing events, Joseph was freed from prison and promoted, becoming the second most powerful man in all Egypt. He held this position during a time of famine that spread beyond Egypt and into Canaan. Joseph's wise management ensured that Egypt had storehouses of grain even as the surrounding areas starved. There was enough, in fact, to feed Egypt and to sell to other lands. In Canaan, Jacob and his family felt the food shortage keenly, so Jacob dispatched ten of his sons to Egypt to bring back grain. The brothers unknowingly came to Joseph asking for food, and through this encounter he revealed his identity. The story ends poignantly with the brothers' repentance and Joseph's forgiveness.

Joseph's story is familiar to many, but it struck us anew after reading a chapter in Edward Miller's book *Letters to the Thirsty*. It tells the story of an extravagant cup and what happened to the brothers through its discovery. Let's backtrack just a bit.

During the first encounter in Egypt, Joseph recognized his brothers and accused them of spying, beginning a test to reveal the state of their hearts (Genesis 42:15). He wanted to guarantee their return to his country, so Joseph put Simeon in custody. He stipulated that in order for them to see him for more grain (and for Simeon's release) on their next trip, they would need to bring their youngest brother, Benjamin, with them.

In time, the family's grain supply dwindled, but the famine did not. Jacob said to his sons, "Go back and buy us a little more food" (43:2). Judah told his aging father that unless Benjamin went with them, there would be no food. Jacob balked at the idea of exposing his remaining favored son to any risk, and Judah, the very one who had suggested selling Joseph in the first place (37:26), now put his own life on the line as guarantee for Benjamin's safe return (43:8-10).

As the brothers appeared before Joseph for the second grain purchase, a curious event occurred. "Deeply moved at the sight of his brother, Joseph hurried out and looked for a place to weep" (43:30). Joseph had forgiven his brothers for selling him to Egypt. He ached to be close to them—to reveal to them who he really was. He loved them deeply, and had acutely felt the loss of his family in all his years away in a strange land. The need to have their grain sacks filled brought them back, but Joseph had far more in mind than soup-kitchen aid—more than his brothers, in their wildest dreams, could have imagined.

And then came the silver cup. Joseph instructed his workers to fill his brothers' sacks with grain and to slip the payment for the food into the mouth of each sack. And Joseph added one more request: "Then put my cup, the silver one, in the mouth of the youngest one's sack along with the silver for his grain" (44:2). Shortly after their departure, Joseph sent his steward to catch them and threaten slavery to the one discovered with the supposedly-stolen cup. When the cup was found in Benjamin's sack, the brothers "tore their clothes" and rushed back to Joseph's presence (44:13). Judah's remorseful, detailed confession and offer to be enslaved in Benjamin's place convinced Joseph of the brothers' deep contrition for their sin against him and their father, Jacob (44:16-33). Only at this point did Joseph reveal his identity, forgiving his brothers and showing them that their deed had not led to evil after all.

At first glance, it seems like Joseph was toying with his brothers—playing a cruel game of cat-and-mouse. Accusing his brothers of stealing the silver cup caused anguish and great fear. Why would Joseph be so cruel to his brothers? Why would he let them go through all the suffering caused by the ploy with the royal cup?

The Gift We Really Need

The pain generated by the royal goblet enabled his brothers to become reacquainted with Joseph. The misery brought his brothers back to Egypt, to his side. The suffering tested their character, revealing what they would do now that a second favored brother, Benjamin, was facing death, just like Joseph had so many years before. Without the ordeal of the silver cup, his brothers would never know Joseph the way he wanted to know them. Edward Miller explains:

> Allow me to rehearse what led to the planting of that wonderful cup. When his brothers came down to Egypt, Joseph was a stranger to them. He loved them and longed for the day he could say, "I am Joseph!" But they were not ready for that yet. Several

times Joseph stole away from their presence to weep in private because he could not tell them who he was. Joseph grieved that his brothers stood before him only because he was the only one who could fill their empty sacks.

And how much more God is grieved when our prayers amount to "take my gift; fill my sack; and dismiss me as a stranger!"

Joseph wanted more than to provide for his family. He also wanted to be no more a stranger to them. If not for the silver cup planted in the sack, they would have departed from Joseph's presence and never known him; but because of it they had to return to him and he could then reveal himself to them. By the silver cup they came to know their provider in a personal way...God loves us too much to allow us to remain strangers.[1]

The parallels between Joseph and our Lord are striking.

Joseph was exceedingly glad to provide ample food for his brothers. God's storehouses are bursting and He wants to meet all of our needs.

Joseph's brothers perceived him (at worst) as a harsh, authoritarian ruler and (at best) as a shrewd grain-dispenser. His brothers had no idea that he knew and loved them intensely. Likewise, many Christians are clueless about God's Father-love. When pain pummels them, many believe God is harsh and uncaring. Others turn to Him merely to meet their physical needs, having settled for a superficial relationship with Him as their grain-dispenser.

Joseph ached to reveal himself to his brothers and to enjoy an intimate family connection. God desires, with greatest passion, to show His kids who He really is. He craves their attention, admiration, and closeness (John 4:23).

Joseph, with the silver cup, intentionally and lovingly caused great inner conflict and chaos to propel his brothers back into his presence. He wanted to see their authentic sorrow and repentance in their lives so that he could move to a deeper level in his relationship with them. God also intentionally uses *silver cups* such as emotional turmoil, financial hardship, interpersonal conflict, disease, and personal losses so that we will nestle ourselves close to Him.

Sometimes suffering is the result of others' sin or the simple existence of ruin and pain in this world. Yet, each event is used by God for our maturing. Joseph did not call down the famine on the land. But through the episode with the silver cup, Joseph utilized the famine to bring his brothers back to a relationship with him. So, too, God uses events that are painful in order for us to need and know Him better.

John White explained, "God hears all poured-out agony, but He longs to be something more than a celestial pacifier. He wants people in their suffering to come to Him. For He is Himself the gift we really need."[2]

For He is the gift we really need. These words illuminate the truth—the evidence that God is not cruel, playing games with the hearts of His helpless children. When the famine struck the land, Joseph knew that his family would be sorely affected. But, he may also have guessed that the old, old pain was still festering in his family—the pain of his disappearance. Did he guess at the guilt and disgust that seethed in his brothers down through the years, as they thought about what they had done? Did he guess at the never-healing wound his father bore, that he could not protect the son he so loved?

To heal such anguish, hours of panic and despair were no price at all to pay.

Pure Joy

In his epistle, James proclaims to Christians what seems to be a paradox. "Consider it pure joy, my brothers, whenever you face trials of many kinds, because you know that the testing of your faith develops perseverance. Perseverance must finish its work so that you may be mature, not lacking anything" (James 1:2-3). The silver cups in this world are permitted in order to develop muscles that otherwise would not be strengthened. Pastor and author Ron Mehl explained this principle clearly seen in the animal world:

> A group of researchers once studied 100 caterpillars which were about to fight their way free from the chrysalis. Instead of letting them struggle, however, the observers gently cut them out and released them. Then they set the insects on a table and tried to get them to fly. But none of them could. Not one.
>
> The study demonstrated that the time of wrestling and fighting through the walls of the cocoon actually strengthens the wings of the butterfly to take flight. The very struggle—all the pushing and thrashing of the insect to free itself from restraint—is what makes its new life possible. Without the strife, there is no strength.[3]

So, too, for us humans—"Without the strife, there is no strength." And all the while, with open arms, our compassionate Father longs for people in pain to rush to Him through prayer. He desires that caregivers and the people they serve embrace the unpleasant silver cups as "pure joy," knowing that each one has been carefully designed by God to beckon us to find comfort at His side.

Still, our silver cups have been filled with a bitter mix that has caused us massive pain. Tammy remembers: My mom faced ill health throughout much of her adult life. Yet, her silver cup of bodily suffering brought her to her Father's side time and again. Her royal mug led her to a sweet intimacy with her heavenly Father. Before her death, Mom carefully printed on a piece of paper the songs and Scripture she wanted at her funeral. On that special day, my sister-in-law lifted her beautiful voice to William Walford's song *Sweet Hour of Prayer*. The words movingly capture the connection between prayer and the silver cups in this world:

> Sweet hour of prayer, sweet hour of prayer,
> That calls me from a world of care,

And bids me at my Father's throne
Make all my wants and wishes known;
In seasons of distress and grief,
My soul has often found relief
And oft escaped the tempter's snare
By thy return, sweet hour of prayer.

For all who have tasted the bitterness and loss drunk from a silver cup, Walford penned the great source of our hope in the last verse:

Till from Mount Pisgah's lofty height,
I view my home, and take my flight;
This robe of flesh I'll drop, and rise
To seize the everlasting prize;
And shout, while passing through the air,
Farewell! Farewell, sweet hour of prayer![4]

A Wild Hope

People throughout history, no matter what their beliefs, have hoped for a Someday that will take them beyond the grief of the world they live in, beyond the bitterness of silver cups and sinking ships. As followers of Christ we have been assured of that Someday. Someday, there will be no more need of the ministry of pain to beckon us to God's side. Are the words of Walford's last verse true? Will we rejoice at the conclusion of our "sweet hour of prayer" one day?

C. S. Lewis responded to this question in the final pages of his Chronicles of Narnia series, during a conversation between the mighty lion Aslan and the children.

Aslan turned to them and said: "You do not yet look so happy as I mean you to be."
Lucy said, "We're so afraid of being sent away, Aslan. And you have sent us back into our own world so often."
"No fear of that," said Aslan. "Have you not guessed?"
Their hearts leaped and a wild hope rose within them.

"There was a real railway accident," said Aslan softly. "Your father and mother and all of you are—as you used to call it in the Shadowlands—dead. The term is over: the holidays have begun. The dream is ended—this is morning."[5]

And as He spoke, He no longer looked to them like a lion; but the things that began to happen after that were so great and beautiful that I cannot write them. And for us this is the end of all stories; and we can most truly say that they all lived happily ever after. But for them it was only the beginning of the real story. All their life in this world and all their adventures in Narnia had only been the cover and the title page: now at last they were beginning Chapter One of the Great Story that no one on earth has read, which goes on forever and in which every chapter is better than the one before.

Reflections

1. Where does pain tend to push you?

2. Edward Miller helped us see that Joseph intentionally placed the silver cup in Benjamin's bag (Genesis 44). This discovery brought a lot of pain, but it also brought his brothers back to Joseph. What have been some silver cups that God has placed in your life?

3. How has He revealed Himself to you in those silver-cup-moments?

Notes

[1] Miller, Edward. *Letters to the Thirsty* (Colorado Springs: WaterBrook Press), 1998, pp. 30-32.

[2] White, John. *Daring to Draw Near: People in Prayer* (Downers Grove, IL: InterVarsity Press), 1977, p. 92.

[3] Mehl, Ron. *God Works the Night Shift* (Sisters, OR: Multnomah Publishers, Inc.), 1994, p. 25.

[4] Walford, William. "Sweet Hour of Prayer," *The Hymnal for Worship and Celebration* (Waco, TX: Word Music), 1986.

[5] Lewis, C. S. *The Chronicles of Narnia: The Last Battle* (New York, NY: C. S. Lewis [Pte] Ltd.), 1984, pp. 210-211.

CHAPTER FIVE

Not the Answer I Was Looking For
Why Does God Keep Us Waiting?

Every war, every famine or plague, almost every deathbed, is the monument to a petition that was not granted. – C. S. Lewis

Between the proverbial rock and the hard place is often the place where God speaks. – Calvin Miller

The man who would know God must give time to Him. – A. W. Tozer

More Than a Train Ticket

A little girl waited on the platform as the huge train puffed and squealed into the station. Her father stood beside her, clutching the train tickets firmly in one hand and the little girl's tiny fingers in the other. As the crowd started to move forward, the child asked her father for her ticket, but he gently told her to wait. Later, as they stepped up onto the train, the father handed the girl the anticipated ticket. He showed her that at precisely her moment of need, he would provide for her. Waiting for the train that day, her father wanted to strengthen her trust in him; and more importantly, he wanted to teach her about the character of God.

Corrie Ten Boom is one of the prayer luminaries of the past century. Her life expressed the texture, color, and shape of what it means to be a praying woman. Standing in a lineup in Ravensbruck concentration camp, Corrie remembered the lesson her father had taught her years before on the platform of a train station, when she had asked him for her ticket. He had taken care of her then just when she needed him, and he had told her that God would do the same, even if he, her earthly father, was no longer there to protect her. Now, in the prison camp, Corrie heard her name called. Names called from the lineup meant execution. How could she face such a merciless death?

As she stepped forward to her death sentence, Corrie whispered goodbye to her prison friends and once more encouraged them to love Jesus even in the midst of evil. As she walked toward the hate-filled guards, she thought of that childhood lesson in the train station. Her loving heavenly Father would provide at her point of need. His grace would be sufficient for her—even in execution.[1]

Corrie was not executed that day. When all hope seemed lost, God provided a way of escape and she lived to walk out of Ravensbruck a free woman. If her father had not taught her the lesson of the train ticket when she was young and safe, how would she have faced the fear that assailed her when she was an adult, and in grave danger? How would she have learned not to despair during her final moments? Corrie's father, though he could not foresee the ordeal ahead of his beloved daughter, had known that she required more than a train ticket that day. He provided for her need, but in his love he did not stop with just the immediate need. The Lord used her father to teach her a lesson of patience and trust so she would come to understand that her Heavenly Father would provide for her just as her earthly father had. Precisely when she needed it.

Close By His Side

Many times we have pleaded with God for answers. We have prayed with desperate people for a spouse to stop cheating, for eyes to see again, for a teenager to give up drugs, for a soldier-son to come home alive, for cancer to be healed. Sometimes we received the answer we were hoping for. Often, we did not. And sometimes we had to wait long years for the answer to come. We know that God is neither powerless, nor careless, nor blind; so why does He allow us to wait when He could answer our prayers as soon as we ask? All those prayers continue to teach us this: God uses the pain in our lives to remind us how much we need Him. *He uses waiting to keep us close by His side.*

A missionary friend in a Muslim country shared a story about waiting in the midst of winter. The cold winter months are a severe trial for countless people. Their poverty denies them the comfort of warm homes, coats, and boots. One mother, whose children were sick because of the cold, told our Christian friend that she had no money for medical care. Our friend helps when she can with clothing and medicine, but resources are soon depleted under the magnitude of human need. She asked this woman if they could talk with God about her need. With delight, the woman agreed and they prayed. Several days later an e-mail arrived from a group back home who wanted to give in some way, knowing nothing of the need. They were sending money—enough for coats and boots! Excitedly, the missionary shared this answer to prayer with her new friend, who wept for joy. God sees all of our needs and He hears as soon as we pray. Sometimes, however, He knows that we will learn more about Himself and His willingness to provide when we pray and then wait. Had our compassionate Christian friend jumped in to help, this Muslim woman would have learned of the missionary's kindness, but may never have discovered that God Himself hears and provides, even when we are called to wait.

When Waiting Seems to Have No Purpose: Roger's Story

I remember her as old and frail. Her husband was an alcoholic. When Nancy and I took the children's group to sing for Emma at Christmas time, they would pause to sing a carol for her husband as he sat clutching his wine bottle. Since cancer had taken Klaus' larynx he spoke with a vibrator against his throat. There had been a time, decades earlier, when for several months he had not spoken a single word to Emma, taking his meals in the bedroom away from the family. Emma turned to God for help. She trusted God for her salvation and for His support to bear the overwhelming burden of an angry, drinking husband.

Klaus fell ill. When Emma walked into the hospital room his eyes opened wide. "You would visit me?" he exclaimed. She came daily. After he returned home, Klaus started eating again with the family. Emma remained kind to him till the end, "through many dangers, toils and snares," though he did not turn to God. Others and I had joined her prayers for him for a few years. She had prayed for decades. And then the call came. "They say he will die soon. Would you visit him one last time?" she asked.

I went to Emma's home to pray with her before going to the hospital. Her words still echo in my ears. Emma said, "I've prayed for forty years for him to believe in Jesus Christ and follow Him. That's all I've wanted." We prayed together one more time for God's miracle.

A five-minute visit was all that was allowed in ICU. Klaus recognized me with a nod, and I shared, again, the greatest story ever to vibrate human eardrums. Christ died to pay the sin-debt of us all—mine and his. I told him he could unload his heavy burden of sin on Jesus and become His follower. Klaus was invited to believe in Christ, to ask Jesus to forgive him and make him His forever child as I prayed. After the "Amen," I gripped his hand, and this dying man uttered the word, "Danke" ("Thank you"). Klaus died the next day.

When We Wait for Rescue and Receive Calamity

Tammy's greatest inheritance is her mother's prayer journals. Some of these tattered notebooks filled with conversations with God have grandchildren's names printed with black felt markers on the front cover. Journals just for them. Other notebooks are lined with words of thanks and passages of Scripture that were whispered to God on behalf of loved ones. Many notebooks are filled with daily requests on behalf of a woman in a grocery-store line, a man on the elevator, a name in the bulletin, and her own pleas for help.

Habakkuk is also a prayer journal. It is unique among other Old Testament books, which were recordings of God's message to the Jews. This little volume contains the dialogue between Habakkuk and his God. It is found among the dustier pages of most Bibles, the Minor Prophets.

Habakkuk lived during grim times. Judah, his nation, was brazenly living as if there were no God. Habakkuk was a wise caregiver. When he was troubled, He talked with God. But it seemed to Habakkuk that God had turned a deaf ear, and he cried heavenward in his distress, "How long, O Lord, must I call for help, but you do not listen? Or cry out to you, 'Violence!' but you do not save?" (1:2). In Judah, strife was everywhere (1:3), justice was perverted, and the wicked had gained the upper hand (1:3-4).

Sounds familiar, doesn't it? We have worked with countless kids who have writhed under one senseless beating after another. To respond to this injustice, Americans look to the court systems. Our search to correct these wrongs is evident as America has more lawyers than any other nation on earth, and we look to the court systems for justice. But fairness is rarely found. Waiting rooms, courtrooms and churches are filled with hurting people who cry out to God for help. Yet in the eyes of too many He seems to do nothing, or He appears to wait far too long.

In this nation filled with injustice Habakkuk, in essence, questioned God, "What are you going to do?" God responded that He had been listening all the while to Habakkuk's cry, and His answer confounded the prophet. God informed Habakkuk that He was raising up an ungodly nation, the Babylonians, to bring justice. Judah and other nations were also going to be crushed by this brutal people "whose own strength is their god" (1:11).

This was not the answer the pleading prophet was expecting! Devastated and confused, Habakkuk asked the age-old question that has shaken the faith of sages and simpletons alike: "Why all this suffering?"

His question was not unique. And his tone was exceptionally harsh, not unlike the weeping prophet Jeremiah, the anguished King David, and perhaps some of us on occasion. What was unique was his response after posing the question. Habakkuk made a choice that lies at the center of this prayer chronicle. He stopped fighting God and climbed a watchtower. Sounds kind of odd, doesn't it? However, in those days, from their perch atop city walls, watchmen could register every movement of friend or foe. Habakkuk climbed to a quiet place free from distraction to wait on God's response to the question of suffering (2:1).

There are bitter times in life when we plead with God for rescue, and we receive calamity instead. God's vision is far-reaching, and His plans are vast; and sometimes the answers seem worse than the need they fill. In these times we are left with few choices. We can become bitter against God. We can decide to leave Him and seek an easier lord. Or we can decide to trust Him until His purpose is revealed...even if it never is. We can leave the city; or we can climb a watchtower and wait.

When God spoke to Habakkuk, He affirmed the prophet's choice to wait and listen. "For the revelation awaits an appointed time...though it linger, wait for it; it will certainly come and not delay" (2:3-4). Disbelief is the ordinary response to pain and waiting. In our nanosecond age, we demand quick answers to confusing hurt. Yet, God is pleased when we learn to wait for Him. Waiting demonstrates that even when our lives are careening out of control, we trust that He is in control. We know His loving and steady hand is on the steering wheel.

God told Habakkuk that He would bring ultimate justice, but Habakkuk needed to wait. Even though it appeared to be the last inning and there seemed to be no way to win, God was still sovereign. Habakkuk would not be around to see the Babylonians *get* it, but God reminded him that the wicked would be punished and His righteous plan *would* prevail. "Woe to him who piles up stolen goods and makes himself wealthy by extortion! How long must this go on?" God demanded of the Babylonians. "Will not your debtors suddenly arise? Will they not wake up and make you tremble? Then you will become their victim. Because you have plundered many nations, the peoples who are left will plunder you" (Habakkuk 2:6-8).

In Hannah Hurnard's classic allegory *Hinds' Feet on High Places*, the main character, Much-Afraid, discovered that lesson which is always easier taught than learned: acceptance-with-joy.[2] Much-Afraid set out on her spiritual journey accompanied by two companions: Sorrow and Suffering. Dismayed at first by the grim guides, Much-Afraid accepted their help because her beloved Great Shepherd asked her to. As the journey progressed, she came to understand that her escorts were necessary in order to help her arrive at the high places of victory and joy. She couldn't have arrived at her final destination without them.

Waiting with longing for the High Places, Much-Afraid was dismayed to find that her path kept turning from the promised mountains—through the scorched desert, past the Sea of Loneliness, and into desolate areas where the High Places were not even in sight. Sorrow and Suffering held her hands and gave her strength to wait out the long miles she had to tread. Much-Afraid discovered the lesson her loving Shepherd wanted her to understand: "All of my servants on their way to the High Places have had to make this detour through the desert...Here they have learned many things that otherwise they would have known nothing about" (p. 85).

Habakkuk's prayer journal concludes with a symphony of praise. On the pinnacle of a watchtower, looking over his doomed city, he was reminded of hope. The hope that God is not neglectful or powerless. His perspective was transformed even though his circumstances grew worse. He would accept the things he couldn't change because He learned that God knew what was best. He gained an understanding that God changes things when we speak with Him. Most often, He changes us.

> Yet I will wait patiently for the day of calamity
> to come on the nation invading us.

> Though the fig tree does not bud
>> and there are no grapes on the vines,
> though the olive crop fails
>> and the fields produce no food,
> though there are no sheep in the pen
>> and no cattle in the stalls,
> yet I will rejoice in the Lord,
>> I will be joyful in God my Savior.
> The Sovereign Lord is my strength;
>> He makes my feet like the feet of a deer,
>> He enables me to go on the heights. (*Habakkuk* 3:16-19)

The average North American does not understand the gravity of withering figs, grapes, and olives. To the Jews of Habakkuk's day, these items were their daily provisions and deeply symbolic. Figs symbolized peace and prosperity and were used for medicine. Grapes produced sugar, wine, and honey. Sheep generated wool for clothing. Cattle meant power to plow the fields.[3] All these life-sustaining resources were vanishing in the drought that gripped Judah. Yet, in the midst of his desolate circumstances, this godly prophet fixed his gaze upon God. Habakkuk, a wise caregiver, realized he could not solve Judah's problems, nor could he avert impending judgment, since the people did not want to change.

Habakkuk had come to realize that *when God gives us what we ask for, it is because He loves us. And when He does not give us what we ask for, it is because He loves us.* This spirit of trust in God's kindness is mirrored in the lyrics of the song, "Blessed Be Your Name."[4] Songwriters Matt and Beth Redman reflect on Job's recognition in Job 1:21 that the Lord gives and the Lord takes away. Nevertheless believers can continue to bless His name.

Those Who Hope in the Lord

Countless people of faith suffered miserable deaths while waiting, without seeing fulfillment (Hebrews 11:35-40). What then does God accomplish by having us wait? What gift does He want to give us in the midst of these difficult times of waiting?

In God's big picture of things, delayed gratification is one of His prime ways of keeping us close to Him so He can mature us. "Perseverance [patience] must finish its work so you may be mature and complete, not lacking anything" (James 1:4). This is a great hope in the midst of our waiting. The prophet Isaiah wrote: "Even youths grow tired and weary, and young men stumble and fall; but those who hope in the Lord [wait upon the Lord, KJV] will renew their strength. They will soar on wings like eagles; they will run and not grow weary, they will walk and not be faint" (Isaiah 40:30-31). The NIV captures the focus of the Hebrew prophet. "Hope in the Lord" is loaded with anticipation, as opposed to killing time passively. When we wait for God to provide for us, we gain endurance and strength we could not otherwise have had.

Chuck Colson explained that God often does not show us the answer to our pleas, this side of heaven. Instead, He tells us to wait. Colson cites more illustrations of people who worked faithfully and trusted God, and could not have known how great a tale they were part of.

> Most of the great figures of the Old Testament died without ever seeing the fulfillment of the promises they relied on. Paul expended himself building the early church, but as his life drew to a close he could see only a string of tiny outposts along the Mediterranean, many weakened by fleshly indulgence or divided over doctrinal disputes…Few were the converts during Hudson Taylor's lifelong mission work in the Orient; but today millions of Chinese embrace the faith he so patiently planted and tended.[5]

Face to Face

As we cry out to God on behalf of hurting people and we teach hurting people to cry out to God, we realize that at times God doesn't change our circumstances. Sometimes, He does bring a spouse back and our kids get off drugs. Occasionally, these answers come swiftly and other times years drag by. At times, it appears that He wants to teach us greater things through delayed answers—to keep us close by His side.

Reflections

1. The prophet Habakkuk wrestled with God and then chose to wait on God for an answer to the question of suffering (Habakkuk 2:1). What are some pain-filled requests for which God has not chosen yet to give you an answer?

2. How have you responded to God while you waited? Why?

3. Ponder these words for a moment: When God gives us what we ask for, it is because He loves us. And when He does not give us what we ask for, it is because He loves us. Do you really believe He loves you when He has kept you waiting?

Notes

[11] Ten Boom, Corrie. *The Hiding Place* (Minneapolis: World Wide Pictures, Inc.), 1975.

[2] Hurnard, Hannah. *Hinds' Feet on High Places* (Wheaton: Tyndale House Publishers, Inc.), 1993.

[3] Briscoe, Jill. *Running on Empty: Refilling your Spirit at the Low Points of Life* (Wheaton: Harold Shaw Publishers), 1995.

[4] Redman, Matt and Beth Redman. "Blessed Be Your Name" (Thankyou Music), 2002.

[5] Colson, Charles. *Loving God* (Grand Rapids: Zondervan Publishing House), 1983, p. 36.

CHAPTER SIX

Prayer Friends
How Can We Give and
Receive Support in Caregiving?

As iron sharpens iron, so one man sharpens another. – Proverbs 27:17

Brothers, pray for us. – Paul (1 Thessalonians 5:25)

Todd Beamer and several other heroes rushed the hijackers of United Flight 93, preventing the plane from crashing into the Capitol, the White House, Camp David, or some other national landmark. On the morning of September 11, 2001, Lisa Beamer received the confirming news from the airline that her husband was on the fatal flight. Lisa, pregnant with their third child, was confronted with the fact that her husband would not be coming through the front door again. She would have to tell her two small children that daddy had died.

Family and friends traveled from around the country to comfort Lisa in her time of grief. Scores of individuals across the world began calling out to God in this time of crisis. One friend in particular quietly called out to Him on Lisa's behalf.

At one point in the middle of the day, during a lull in the activity in my room, I was staring blankly into space. I looked across Todd's and my bed, and there was Jan Pittas, one of our more quiet-natured friends, just sitting on the opposite corner of the bed, quietly praying for me, not talking aloud. Not talking at all. I didn't want to talk; I wasn't able to talk. And with her sweet, gentle spirit, Jan knew better than to try to talk to me. But her presence in the room was comforting."

"Thank you, God, for sending Jan, I prayed."[1]

A Praying Friend: Roger's Story

Coming back to the United States after twenty years of ministry in Germany was, in many ways, a difficult transition. One of the greatest trials was losing the support I had enjoyed from a terrific team of praying ministry friends. Back in the States, I felt their absence like a gaping wound. Deep concern careened toward panic as the hunger for a close friend and prayer partner grew. So I asked God for a praying friend.

One day, while sitting in the office of my teaching colleague, Ken, it dawned on me that God had answered my request. Now fifteen years later, we both treasure our times of deep sharing and prayer. Often the planned ten minutes turn into an hour. Sometimes Ken lacks perspective; other times I need encouragement; and we both could always use a laugh, and the assurance of friendship and support. I wouldn't want to imagine my life without this trusted, praying man. We know each other profoundly, call on God for each other's concerns, confront wrong attitudes, cheer about mutual victories, and high-five at the birth of beautiful grandchildren!

Does this companionship between Ken and me remind you of a friend in your own life? Tammy and I suspect that for many this type of trusting, prayer-centered relationship sounds unlikely, even implausible. We sense that it is a tragically small number of men and women who have a friend with whom they can pray consistently and spontaneously—for any concern, joy, pain, or desire. How many caregivers have no one to pray for them during the hours they spend with hurting and hurtful people?

To Find Strength in God

David and Jonathan are the archetype of friendship. These men remained friends through war, exile, and the death of Israel's first royal dynasty. Jonathan, the son of the king, was David's best friend; and when David fell out of favor with the king, their friendship did not falter.

King Saul was a man festering with jealousy over the praise Israel awarded to David, a simple shepherd-boy-turned-warrior. The people liked Saul, but they loved David; and their partiality infuriated Saul. He turned on David, whom he had once praised, and his rage drove him to pursue David "day after day" (1 Samuel 23:14) with the intent of killing him. Saul became David's "enemy the rest of his days" (1 Samuel 18:29). David was forced to put his mother and father into hiding (22:3). He fled to the desert, surviving by moving from cave to cave, and lived as a fugitive in constant danger of capture. It was a grim time for David, outnumbered and pursued, never able to drop his guard. In the midst of the assault, David pleaded with God for help (23:16).

Then we read about help arriving from Jonathan, the best of friends. Even though Jonathan was caught between David and Dad, he risked death to seek out David at Horesh and encourage his broken friend. During this dark time, Jonathan gave the most loving gift a friend could give—he directed David's face toward God. What could Jonathan say to David in the face of his own father's brutality? What could he say to the man he already knew was destined to inherit the kingship, instead of Jonathan himself (1 Samuel 23:17)? He did not try to comfort David with his own compassion, or with assurances that it would all be okay; instead, "Saul's son Jonathan went to David at Horesh and helped him find strength in God" (1 Samuel 23:16).

Their encounter illustrates the essence of what a caregiver is meant to be, and what a caregiver needs in order to fulfill his or her calling. Fledgling caregivers often attempt to explain the reason for distressed people's difficult circumstances. Trite platitudes are shuffled and dealt. Our comforting words are empty to people who are still on the run in the desert. Jonathan, by contrast, did not try to interpret the why of David's situation. Nor did he make empty promises that it would all be over soon, or that Saul would come around. Instead, he directed David to the arms of God, where David found strength. Notice that God's Word did not say, "Jonathan helped David find strength in Jonathan's skilled interventions, empathy, and good advice" (although he was probably gifted in each of these ways). Jonathan gave the greater gift. He became a signpost to God.

We have a fellow professor who experienced this recently in the middle of a wedding reception. He kindly wrote about it for us:

> I have taught psychology at a Christian college for almost 30 years. Nothing in my professional experience had prepared me, however, for the shock when the results of a recent test pointed to a possible aggressive form of leukemia in my body.
>
> Not long after being hit with this discouraging news, I attended the wedding of two of my former students. In spite of the happy celebration around me, I was anything but joyful—wondering about possible bone marrow transplants and whether I would live to see my grandchildren's weddings.
>
> During the wedding reception, one of the groomsmen, also a former student, approached me and asked how I was doing. I told him both of my diagnosis and the preliminary test data.
>
> Surrounded by a noisy, celebrating crowd and loud music, this young man put his arm around me

and said, "I want to pray for you right now." What followed was a tender, eloquent prayer, expressing appreciation for me and requesting my healing. When he finished the prayer, he turned to me and said, "I love you."

We parted, after an embrace. A big lump filled my throat. My praying friend had encouraged my heart and reminded me of God's love in a way that I don't believe could have happened as well through any other circumstances. No one has ever seen God but sometimes we get fuzzy glimpses of Him through those who reflect His love.

When you are at the bottom of your pit or in the midst of your desert, who listens, loves, and points you to God? The ministry of caregiving is full of low moments and points of despair. I (Roger) remember sitting one hour with a couple in crisis; the husband was bent on divorce. After gentle prodding, confrontation, and earnest pleading to God, the man still responded, "Divorce is the only answer. She is incurably ill and I need my freedom." *Like the kind of freedom a high-diver gets jumping into an empty pool*, I thought. Another hour was spent in a conversation with a Christian leader who had been caught knee-deep in pornography. These types of situations leave us drained and discouraged. Working with hurting and hurtful people brings a unique sadness and a sapping fatigue. How can we face these aches single-handedly?

I'll Go to Battle; You Go Seek God

One of our favorite scenes depicting the importance of Christian caregivers having spiritual support is found nestled in the book of Exodus. In chapter 17, Moses stands upon the crest of a hill silhouetted against the sky; his arms are raised, and he bears a staff in his hand. He is looking to God for help. Far below, Joshua leads the Israelites in battle. Moses carries no sword or spear. He has no written, tactical strategy. He has no radio to transmit orders to the fighting men below. Instead, while General Joshua fought, Moses' "hands were lifted to the throne of the LORD" (v. 16). Several commentators believe that Moses was praying with uplifted hands (see Exodus 9:29).

"As long as Moses held up his hands, the Israelites were winning, but whenever he lowered his hands, the Amalekites were winning" (v. 11). As the soldiers in the battle below looked upward, they could see their leader, who had led them through desert and sea, through peril and doubt; and he was standing before God for them (v. 9). And they knew that God saw him, and because of his faithfulness was giving them the victory. What an inspiring scene!

Moses expected God to deliver the people. God saw his heart of trust and gave victory as long as his hands were raised. Have you ever been around a person who talks with God as regularly as sunrise— someone who pours out his soul and realizes every breath depends on the God of the universe? Moses was a potent person of prayer like that. He was the kind of praying leader James talked about when he said, "The prayer of a righteous man is powerful and effective" (James 5:16). Moses knew implicitly that while a battle was going on below, another battle raged on the hilltop and in the heavens.

Sometimes prayer seems effortless. During such times, all we want to do is spend time with our Lord. And then there are desert seasons when pleading with God is a difficult spiritual battle. There came a point, as Moses was praying for the soldiers of Israel, that his arms became rubbery and he could no longer hold them up (Exodus 17:12). When Moses was faint with weariness, Aaron and Hur came along and literally "held his hands up—one on one side, one on the other—so that his hands remained steady till sunset" (v. 13).

If the Israelites had fought alone that day, they would have been scattered and defeated. If Moses had borne a sword on the battlefield instead of a staff on the hill, they would have been lost. What modern soldier would march alone into battle without knowing that supply lines were functioning and a radio was handy to call for help? In our spiritual walk we know that help from God is vital to our survival, just as the continuation of supply lines is essential to the survival of soldiers. What missionary would hustle off to Hong Kong without pleading for God's people to pray for her? What pastor preaches week after week without being supported in prayer? Few, if they truly understand that spiritual power comes only from God.

Yet, ask any number of Christian counselors who it is that prays daily for them as they meet with hurting people. Who provides their spiritual supply line? Who holds up the staff for them as they do battle with sin and despair? Who intercedes for them, not simply praying for their well-being, their marriage, children, and health, but who intercedes as they sit with hurting people hour after hour? Tammy has discovered a distressing reality through her conversations with counselors throughout the U.S. and Canada: the vast majority has nobody praying for them as they are in the thick of battle!

Praying Shawnie

I (Tammy) wanted to pass on to my nine-year-old niece the greatest inheritance I received from my mom, praying for others. I called Shawnie, and asked her if she would be one of my prayer partners. I received a post-card with a large cat on it (Shawnie knows how to pick the best postcards!) with her printed reply. "Dear Aunt Tammy, I would love to be your prayer friend." To a nine-year-old, the term "prayer partner" didn't mean much, but prayer friend said it all. Aaron and Hur were Moses' prayer friends.

Moses' task was to lift his hands to the throne of God on behalf of Israel. But even this powerful praying man couldn't do it alone. He needed the support of his prayer friends. Can you see the comparison? Counseling is a battleground. People are fighting in the trenches with alcohol, affairs, abuse, pornography, grief, greed, and all the vast array of sins and tragedies that besiege humanity. Caregivers cannot win the battle. They cannot change lives on their own. Neither can people win the battles in their own lives when they fight alone. Caregivers and those they care for need to be trained well for battle, like Joshua. But they also need a team like Moses, Aaron, and Hur standing on a hill interceding on their behalf.

What would have happened if Moses had not prayed that day? Israel would have lost the war and many lives. What occurs when caregivers have no one praying for them as they counsel?

Stay Here and Keep Watch With Me

Our vision is to see all Christian caregivers build a team of prayer friends dedicated to praying for them as they intervene in people's lives. How many more marriages could be saved, more addicts freed, more grieving comforted, more destructive patterns and abuse stopped, if serious prayer support were given for the battle? How many more caregivers would joyfully spend their lives giving to others, instead of feeling discouraged and used up?

Isn't it interesting that the greatest spiritual leaders are the ones who ask for the most prayer support? The strongest men and women of God most fully realize their need for God and the prayers of their friends. In my (Roger) Principles and Practice of Prayer class, students examine the legendary Apostle Paul's requests for prayer. In five passages (Romans 15:30-33; Ephesians 6:18-20; Colossians 4:2-4; 1 Thessalonians 5:25; 2 Thessalonians 3:1-2) Paul asks his friends to intercede for him. The students are to discover what he asked people to pray for, and to compare or contrast that with the prayer requests often given today.

Students notice that Paul asked his friends to "join me in my struggle by praying to God for me" (Romans 15:30). Evidently the godly leader, Paul, believed that when his friends prayed for him, they were fighting in the trenches with him. Students point out that he asks twice in one context (Ephesians 6:19-20) for his readers to pray for his boldness or fearlessness in speaking God's good news. Another time for God's message to spread rapidly (2 Thessalonians 3:1). Paul urgently desired prayer support for his clear and effective communication (Colossians 4:3-4).

The Lord Jesus, our greatest example of steely strength and deep humility, asked for the prayer support of His disciples as He faced His hour of greatest sorrow and agony, on the night He was arrested. "Then Jesus went with his disciples to a place called Gethsemane, and he said to them, 'Sit here while I go over there and pray.' He took Peter and the two sons of Zebedee along with him, and he began to be sorrowful and troubled. Then he said to them, 'My soul is overwhelmed with sorrow to the point of death. Stay here and keep watch with me'" (Matthew 26:36-38).

On this most momentous and painful of nights, Jesus did not want to be alone. Despite His closeness with His Heavenly Father, He still wanted to have His friends near Him. "Going a little farther, he fell with his face to the ground and prayed, 'My Father, if it is possible, may this cup be taken from me. Yet not as I will, but as you will'" (26:39). We can hear the throbbing ache recorded in Scripture when we read, "Then he returned to his disciples and found them sleeping. 'Could you men not keep watch with me for one hour?' he asked Peter" (Matthew 26:40). Even as He prayed to His Father, Jesus did not want to be forgotten by His friends.

Caregivers, like Paul, need godly wisdom to speak truth at just the right moment, a teachable moment. Like Christ in Gethsemane, we need human companionship and support in prayer even as we walk with our God. Paul and Jesus, who constantly prayed for others, also asked others to pray for them. This was not self-centeredness. May we follow their example by praying constantly for others as well as asking others to pray for us. Being in spiritual solitary confinement is torture. How many caregivers feel the agony of struggling alone with hurting people?

Just as this chapter was being written, I (Tammy) encouraged Roger with a printed copy of an e-mail he had sent out years ago requesting prayer for the seminary. I had forwarded the e-mail to my mother, who had written her conversation to God for his requests in the margins of the printout, and then placed it in one of her prayer notebooks. I just discovered it that very week, six years later! Roger and my mother didn't know one another and never met, yet she prayed faithfully for his requests. That is humbling and uplifting. Her arms were raised on behalf of the seminary.

How Should We Pray?

What specific things should we ask for as we pray for our friends who give counsel? Our Lord presented an example when He prayed for His disciples the night before He was crucified: "I have revealed you to those whom you gave me out of the world. ... I pray for them. I am not praying for the world, but for those you have given me, for they are yours," Jesus said to His Father in John 17:7, 9. He prayed for their protection: "I will remain in the world no longer, but they are still in the world, and I am coming to you. Holy Father, protect them by the power of your name—the name you gave me—so that they may be one as we are one" (v. 11). He prayed for their joy: "I am coming to you now, but I say these things while I am still in the world, so that they may have the full measure of my joy within them" (v. 13).

He prayed for their purity: "They are not of the world, even as I am not of it. Sanctify them by the truth; your word is truth" (vv. 16-17). Jesus was also concerned for everyone who would come to follow Him as a result of their ministry: "My prayer is not for them alone. I pray also for those who will believe in me through their message" (v. 20). These are powerful, practical requests that we can lift up on behalf of the caregivers we know. Notice, none of these requests shared by a caregiver would break confidentiality!

Wouldn't it be amazing if every Christian lawyer, pilot, teacher, and mom would build a team of prayer friends as well?

Ocean-spanning Prayers: Roger's Story

In my eyes they were angels, all of them. Claudia Leffingwell led this vibrant group of elderly ladies, most of them widows. They prayed for cross-cultural servants around the world from Bellflower, California, where one of our supporting churches was located. Their requests to God were specific, regular, and expectant. Claudia often prayed from just after breakfast until lunchtime, with letters spread across her table.

In late 1980, Esther,* about 20, started attending our church in Stuttgart, Germany. She was struggling with a number of issues. Nancy and I asked Claudia and her prayer friends to pray for Esther. In every one of their monthly letters, the ladies asked how Esther was doing and assured us they had been praying. There were many spiritual attacks in Esther's life—a few ups, a lot of downs. Claudia and her team prayed in California, and, in Germany, Nancy and I gave love and counsel and provided accountability to this dear young woman. For six years, this prayer and counseling partnership across an ocean labored for God's intervention in Esther's life.

One day, Esther came to my office to say she was leaving the Christian faith, turning from God. "It's too hard to follow God," she said. As she turned to leave I began sobbing. She paused. I said, "Christ has done so much for you. You cannot simply turn your back on Him."

"I didn't know you cared so much," she replied, and in that moment God captured her heart. Not long after, a Bible school music team visited the church. A young man from the team saw Esther in the crowd and made a beeline for her after the meeting. A beautiful relationship developed. To assist in performing their wedding was one of my happiest ministry events during my time in Germany. Esther's husband is now a church leader. They have three beautiful children who are being raised to honor Christ with their lives.

Most of that Bellflower prayer team are already in heaven. But the effect of years of their "prayer friend" intercession lives on in a precious family in Germany. To uphold a staff, and uphold a battle; to enter the land of exile and help our friends find strength in God; to stay and watch with someone facing loss and great pain—this is what we do when we pray. Our efforts are often invisible, but they are never in vain.

*Not her real name

Reflections

1. Jonathan helped David "find strength in God" (1 Samuel 23:16). Think about someone who helped you find strength in God and describe how they did it.

2. As a caregiver (pastor, psychologist, mom) what steps can you undertake to develop a team of prayer friends?

3. Who are some caregivers for whom you can begin to pray consistently?

Notes

[1] Beamer, Lisa. *Let's Roll!* (Wheaton, IL: Tyndale House Publishers), 2002, pp. 169-170.

CHAPTER SEVEN

How Can We Counsel Non-Christians
(and Others Who Do Not Want to Discuss God)?

If we truly love people, we will desire for them far more than it is within our power to give them, and this will lead us to prayer. – Richard Foster

The Big Question: Tammy's Story

Five-year-old Tommy snapped a leash to Zan's collar and followed the black Labrador Retriever to the door. On an early St. Louis summer morning before his mom and dad awoke, he and "Aunt Tammy" had decided to take Zan for a walk (or more accurately, the powerful beast decided to walk us!). Zan was no obedience school poster dog, and she tugged with all her might, while I gripped the leash and floundered in her wake.

Halfway through the workout, Tommy asked somberly if he could talk to me about something when we got home. The counselor alarm began to buzz in my head. Why didn't Tommy want to talk about his concerns as we trudged through the St. Louis suburb? What was so difficult for him to talk about? Had someone hurt Tommy? He knew his aunt talked with troubled kids and adults about problems in their lives. I wondered what was troubling my five-year-old nephew. Without hesitation and with some concern, I replied, "Of course we can talk."

As Zan was released to the rough country of the back yard, the precocious boy directed me to set up a couple of lawn chairs on the front porch while he got us something to drink. A few minutes later, on that already 90-plus degree day, sipping frosty glasses of iced tea, I gently broached the subject: "Sweetheart, what is it you wanted to talk with me about?"

"Aunt Tammy...," Tommy began slowly, with the serious tone that indicates troubling thoughts. "Who is your favorite superhero?"

I didn't see this question coming. I was not expecting that the unease of this five-year-old boy would center around the virtues and limitations of Batman and Superman! I didn't know quite how to respond. Once I had gotten my mind into the correct context, I told my nephew that Cat Woman, of course, was my favorite superhero. This, apparently, was not an acceptable answer. Tommy gave me his "Come on, Aunt Tammy" look and informed me that Cat Woman was a villain and not a superhero. I hadn't been prepared for Tommy's question, so I didn't have an answer for him.

During sessions with those they counsel, caregivers often are blindsided and aren't sure how to respond wisely to people's biggest concerns. The difficulty is often greatest when we are working with people who don't know God. The gap between a non-Christian and a Christian can be even greater than the gap between a five-year-old boy and his flabbergasted aunt. People who do not share our most important relationship and our most foundational beliefs will often ask questions that we can't anticipate, initiated by an entirely different sense of what is important and what is true. How, then, do Christian caregivers working in secular settings prudently interact with hurting people? How do Christian counselors wisely lead people one step closer to Jesus in non-Christian or even anti-Christian settings?

Too many times to count, we have sat across from both non-Christian and Christian folks who say "I want a divorce," "I am getting an abortion," or "I am moving in with my boyfriend so we can get to know each other better." How do you respond when God's Word means little to the person you are sitting with? What does it mean to be wise in these situations?

He Must Become Greater

Perhaps we can glean some wisdom from a man to whom Jesus gave a high honor: "Among those born of women there has not risen anyone greater than John the Baptist" (Matthew 11:11). John wielded tremendous influence over a whole nation of people who had turned from serving God. What was the key to his impact on unbelievers?

John the Baptist was gifted, bold, and wildly popular. He was clothed in camel's hair garments and crunched meals of locusts and wild honey (Matthew 3:4); and he probably didn't fit the mold for the typical preacher of his day. Yet people came to him and their lives were drastically altered (Matthew 3:5-6).

And then came Jesus. Now there were two men—both teaching and baptizing. It wasn't long before loyal followers of John became angry about the apparent competition. "They came to John and said to him, 'Rabbi, that man who was with you on the other side of the Jordan—the one you testified about—well, he is baptizing, and everyone is going to him'" (John 3:26).

John's response was startling in its humility and wisdom. "He must become greater; I must become less. The one who comes from above is above all" (John 3:30-31). John's followers had failed to understand his intention. His mission was not to bring the focus or honor to himself, or even just to minister to the Judeans. His purpose was to direct people to Jesus. He was preparing the way for someone who would come later. He was helping people to become dedicated to their God again, so that they would be ready when He showed up in person—in the person of Jesus. Matthew 3:3 tells us that "This is he who was spoken of through the prophet Isaiah: 'A voice of one calling in the desert, "Prepare the way for the Lord, make straight paths for him."'"

We believe the mission for Christian caregivers is the same—to draw hurting people one step closer to Jesus! When we walk with hurting people, spending most of our time focusing on symptom reduction, it is like stomping out a campfire when the whole forest is ablaze. Only God can save and heal people. We can help people prepare their hearts, so when He comes to knock on the doors of their lives, they recognize Him, and let Him in.

No One Ever Spoke the Way This Man Does

Our goal as Christian caregivers, then, is to be a signpost to Christ. We can do this, like John the Baptist, aiming others to Him. We strike a dilemma, however, when we try to draw people to God and find they do not want to go. The American Counseling Association's Code of Ethics (1995) is crystal clear when it states, "Counselors are aware of their own values, attitudes, beliefs, and behaviors and how these apply in a diverse society, and avoid imposing their values on clients."[1] We agree. It is unethical and hurtful for a caregiver to arm-wrestle hurting folks into adopting the counselor's beliefs. How then do we help those who come to us, in the way we believe they most need help? How can we invite people to Christ, instead of trying to drag them?

Christian counselors must be aware of their own values and take their cue from the One who modeled those values in His life. The amazing influential power of Christ's words resulted from the overflow of His relationship with His Father. Even those who opposed His message were astonished by the power of the life He lived and the words He spoke. At the trial of Christ, Pilate found "no basis for a charge against him" (John 19:4). Just moments after

Christ's death, the Roman Centurion remarked: "Surely this was a righteous man" (Luke 23:47). Jesus' life was so well-lived that the only accusations of wrongdoing which could be made against Him at His trial were false (Matthew 26:59)! When Christ spoke, His words were compelling and blazing with light. When the temple guards, against the will of the chief priests, failed to arrest Jesus, they were pressed to give a reason. Their reply? "No one ever spoke the way this man does" (John 7:46).

The effect of Christ's presence was most notably apparent in His disciples. Jesus had chosen twelve men "that they might be with him" (Mark 3:14) They were His inner circle and nearly constant companions. Living three years in His immediate presence left the mark of Jesus on these men. After His death, resurrection, and ascension, Peter and John were being interrogated by the ruling Jewish body, and "When they saw the courage of Peter and John and realized that they were unschooled, ordinary men, they were astonished and they took note that these men had been with Jesus" (Acts 4:13).

So, too, the more time we spend with Jesus, the more we come to resemble Him. As we sit with hurting people, we want to wear the mark of His presence so they know we have been with Him. But this does not mean we are to push our agenda and bombard vulnerable folks with Christian values. In fact, we hurt them when we do so. We want to invite people to come to know Him. The appeal of our lives ought to attract individuals to Jesus. The more time we spend with Him, the more our presence tells of a wonderful Person to whom we can point the way.

A Gentle and Quiet Spirit

What, then, does this spirit look like—the kind of spirit that invites and attracts? It is not an aggressive, argumentative, or pushy spirit. It is not a spirit that tries to talk people into following Christ. More often than not, our words should be few. In 1 Peter 3, a married woman who came to know Jesus through the ministry of the apostles wanted to know how to win her husband to Him. Peter instructed her, "Your beauty should not come from outward adornment, such as braided hair and the wearing of gold jewelry and fine clothes. Instead, it should be that of your inner self, the unfading beauty of a gentle and quiet spirit, which is of great worth in God's sight" (1 Peter 3:3-4).

An unbelieving husband will observe the "gentle and quiet spirit" in his now-believing wife, and he will contrast her peace and composure with her previous fretful, sullen, or furious responses. Often the closer the relationship, the fewer words should be used— and fewer words are necessary. When a newly-believing wife leaves Christian books around the house and places gospel pamphlets in her unbelieving husband's lunch bag, it produces the impression that he, as an unbeliever, is not good enough, and that he is now second-rate. This makes him feel rejected and insecure.

The call to possess the "gentle and quiet spirit" Peter writes of is not gender-specific or confined to marriage relationships. Both men and women in all kinds of roles are called to be gentle and humble, instead of aggressive or accusatory. Matthew wrote of Jesus: "I will put my Spirit on him, and he will proclaim justice to the nations. He will not quarrel or cry out; no one will hear his voice in the streets. A bruised reed he will not break, and a smoldering wick he will not snuff out..." (Matthew 12:18-20, quoting Isaiah 42:1-3).

Yet for all His quiet gentleness, Jesus was not weak or spineless. He spoke truth even when it lost Him support and followers (cf. John 6:43-60). He did not flee His task when He was tried and executed. He never tried to smooth things over with the ruling priests in order to save Himself. The gentleness of Jesus is the gentleness of strength, which does not need to prove itself through violence or argument.

Sometimes Christian caregivers need to challenge clients firmly. Gentleness and quietness, however, are often the wiser teachers. A pastoral counselor facing a fuming anti-Christian husband is wise not to fight fire with fire, but instead carefully select his words. A wise counselor does not rise to the bait that an angry client offers. When we are confident that God is who He says He is, this quiet confidence frees us from the need to win arguments about our faith.

A Christian counselor who is employed in a secular mental health center, like the wife of 1 Peter 3:1-4, may be unable to discuss Christian principles during anger management groups or in individual therapy. Still, the caregiver can exhibit compassion and relay wisdom without directly quoting a verse of Scripture. "Pleasant words are a honeycomb, sweet to the soul and healing to the bones" (Proverbs 16:24). "The words of a man's mouth are deep waters, but the fountain of wisdom is a bubbling brook" (Proverbs 18:4). If a caregiver lives his or her life the way Christ lived His, people will be drawn to the caregiver the way they were drawn to Christ. The character of God is winsome and lovely, and it attracts even those who do not know where it comes from.

Going to Extremes

Living the way Christ did, with both gentleness and strength, is a difficult balance. It is hard for us, with our natural tendencies, not to swing too far to one extreme or the other. There are two ways counselors can go to extremes when they are speaking with people who do not share our faith, and thus miss the goal of having a quiet and gentle spirit. One way has been taken by scores of Christian caregivers, especially in secular mental health centers. They become more secularized rather than more discerning. Counselors who take this extreme learn how to diagnose individuals accurately. They become skilled at creating treatment plans. They develop provocative questions to discuss in group therapy. But they stop calling on God for His help even when relationships are failing all around them. They are settling for a focus on symptom-reduction and the changing of circumstances, rather than calling people to come closer to the Healer.

Other Christian caregivers aren't becoming more secularized, but more obnoxious—pushing their faith on unwary nonbelievers. They try to hog-tie and drag non-Christians into the Kingdom of

God. During intake sessions, they unwisely echo John the Baptist with words like "You brood of vipers!" (Matthew 3:7). There is a reason why supervisors want to give them "the right foot of fellowship" when they copy John's candor. His message and method were tailored to the nation of Israel at a specific time in history, when God had prepared Jewish hearts to embrace his directness. The relevance of the content and form of presentation to his particular audience demonstrated his wisdom— not the specifics of word choice and confrontational style. These same elements, when applied to the wrong audience, are no longer wise.

Christian caregivers are called to be wise. Most of the hurting people who come into counseling centers will not feel convicted by a harsh confrontation; they will feel insulted or attacked. Most of these same people would feel much safer and more loved by an invitation—a summons to know Him. Hurting people are thirsty, and Christian caregivers are called to help them become aware of their craving and then direct them, never pushing, to the One who quenches thirst.

Through Many Hardships: Tammy's Story

Being out of step with the cadence of the world means there will be some who are not fond of Christian caregivers even when we display a quiet and gentle spirit. As I was applying for a doctoral internship position at university counseling centers in Canada and the United States, one agency presented me with a provocative ethical dilemma. I was informed that the center was gay-affirming and that the last Christian counselor had difficulty working there because of this fact.

During a second interview with the same agency, I was asked how I would respond to a gay client, if after watching a religious television show he wanted to receive reparative therapy (i.e., therapy that helps individuals come out of the gay lifestyle). I wanted to express my love and concern for homosexuals and to point them to Jesus who loves them more than I do. I also wanted never to compromise what I believed God says about the acting out of homosexual desires. However, it didn't take a Ph.D. to discern that the interviewers were none too fond of reparative therapy and not crazy about any caregiver who might have an affinity toward this intervention. I can spot a set-up when it's waving in the wind.

Opposition facing Christians is not a new problem. Followers of God through the centuries of the Old and New Testaments faced constant opposition, ridicule, and persecution. Tens of thousands since the Church was founded at Pentecost have been opposed, rejected, hated, beaten, and burned, simply because they were followers of Jesus. The Apostle Paul explicitly told new believers, after he himself had been stoned on his first missionary journey, that "we must go through many hardships to enter the kingdom of God" (Acts 14:22).

Even when we do all we can to live as Christ did—with a gentle, compassionate strength—sometimes it will still seem as if our efforts are in vain. There will be times when the people we serve will reject Christ and dismiss our counsel, or when our coworkers will not be drawn to our faith but repulsed by it. It is easy in those moments to lose hope. Our prayer for you is that you will take heart! Jesus also was persecuted for the truth He spoke; His apostles were rejected and martyred. But they changed the face of the world forever.

None of Your God-Talk: Tammy's Story

"I don't want to talk about God," Jon barked during his first session. A man in his late twenties, Jon was tense and agitated. I nodded in acceptance. I had worked in a couple of university counseling centers, a Christian counseling center, private practice, and a secular community mental health center. I knew it wasn't my job to arm-wrestle people into talking about God. Someone once said that trying to change another person is like trying to teach a bull to sing: You can't do it and it irritates the bull. Who was I to wave a red flag in front of this man? I sparked his heated words when I shared that I taught at a Christian college while counseling part time. Jon wanted me to know that there would be no God-talk. He had received Christian counseling in the past and he didn't like it.

In many settings and situations, caregivers don't have the permission to speak of God, or to pray out loud. But we always have the privilege of praying silently—asking God for opportunities to share His love and to lead people to Him—according to His timetable, not ours. So I silently asked for God's help with Jon, who was angry at Christian counselors and the world.

Jon had an antipathy for his job and even more so for his meaningless life. He had floated from one occupation and one relationship to the next. As time marched on, the odd thing was that at some point in each session, this quick-tempered man kept leading the conversation back to God. So I followed and quietly prayed. There was no formula to use and no arguments to raise; so we continued to meet, and I continued to pray.

Over time, Jon returned to church and, most importantly, to the arms of his loving heavenly Father. I later discovered he had a praying mom who had been on her knees for years on behalf of her wayward son, praying that he would return to God.

During a closing hour, still wrestling but walking toward God, he said, "Tammy, you knew all along that was where I needed to be. Thanks for not pushing me." And I once again said silently, "Thanks Father."

Reflections

1. There are many horror stories of Christians who have been overly aggressive in seeking to cram God's Word down the throats of unwilling listeners. Think of an example when you have witnessed a caregiver gently and wisely share the love of Jesus with a hurting person.

2. What traits stand out in the life of this above-named individual which you consider worth emulating?

3. Do you tend to be too aggressive in pushing your agenda on others? Or do you tend to be passive or afraid to share God's good news with broken individuals?

4. Wherever you are on the continuum, will you begin to pray about becoming a caregiver who helps people find strength in God?

Notes

[1] American Counseling Association. *Code of Ethics and Standards of Practice.* (Alexandria, VA), 1998.

CHAPTER EIGHT

Beauty Instead of Ashes
What Does True Transformation Look Like?

*Psychological, social, and political revolutions have not been able to
transform the heart of darkness that lies deep in the breast of every human
being. Amid a flood of self-fulfillment, there is an epidemic of depression,
suicide, personal emptiness, and escapism...So obviously the problem is a
spiritual one. And so must be the cure.* – Dallas Willard

Mere improvement is not redemption. – C. S. Lewis

*To comfort all who mourn, and provide for those who grieve in Zion—to
bestow on them a crown of beauty instead of ashes, the oil of gladness instead
of mourning, and a garment of praise instead of despair. They will be called
oaks of righteousness, a planting of the Lord for the display of his splendor.*
– Isaiah 61:2-3

Clean Sweep

"Unhand that puffy dress!" Flinching, the offending dress
owner ducked behind a clothes rack, gripping a frilly, out-of-style

monstrosity and trying to decide whether to laugh or cry. The command came from a co-host of TLC's *What Not to Wear*, one of TV's many "makeover" programs that a few years ago elbowed sitcoms out of the television lineups.[1] Personal makeovers, career renovations, home transformations—the American audience loved watching the uninspiring or the downright hideous made new.

Another reality show, *Clean Sweep*, focuses on homes filled to the ceilings with stuff; the houses are then cleaned out, neatened up, and redecorated.[2] At the outset of the show, homeowners and the crew of *Clean Sweep* cart mountains of clutter to the yard. Inside, interior designers and carpenters work diligently painting, building, and creating stylish rooms. Outside, an organizer helps homeowners sort through the clutter in order to keep the essentials and rid themselves of the outdated, the unneeded, and the unidentifiable.

Despite the remarkable difference between the original chaos and the promise of beautiful, renovated rooms soon to be revealed, each episode shows that people don't like to get rid of their things. They grip items tightly. Letting go of them is painful. At the end of each show, after home-owners have chosen to give up their boxes of clutter, the hosts reveal the transformed rooms. Homeowners weep, cheer, or stand in awed silence to see the loveliness that is now theirs.

There is something fascinating about seeing such a transformation. Some part of us is delighted when something marred is remade into something beautiful. Yet despite our love of renewal, few of us would do any better than the homeowners featured on the shows, who weep over their ancient magazines and reindeer-embroidered sweaters. The desire to hold onto what is familiar seems to be a deeply-rooted and universal trait.

God longs to do a clean sweep in our lives, but it is difficult for us to get rid of our stuff, even though it is crowding us, choking us, killing us. As caregivers, we can't make anyone clean out their homes or hearts. True transformation is a gift from God. Jesus said, "Apart from me you can do nothing" (John 15:5).

Christmas Miracles and a Taste of Transformation

Rummaging through any bookstore will reveal stacks of books dealing with personal improvement, offering advice on how to change for the better. Many of them are helpful. In numerous cases, however, ten-step cures are short-lived and short-sighted. Human beings are much better at describing problems that need to be changed than they are at making the changes. It's nothing new for experts and pundits to describe what true transformation should look like; but a clear vision of the needed change does not bring that change about. A wise John Daniel Jones, born in 1865, explained.

> There are plenty of people who can diagnose the condition of mankind today with exactness, who can point out the ill and describe the malady, but they can do nothing to redeem people because they know no cure. Thomas Hardy can describe with terrible fidelity man's misery and woe, but he can do little to redeem them.[3]

So what does transformation look like in a world of suffering? What does it mean to overcome the pains of the past?

Literature is replete with examples of transformation in the lives of people. Ebenezer Scrooge in Charles Dickens' *A Christmas Carol* lived a cold life and became a cold man. Despite great wealth and success in his business, Scrooge was a miserable old sinner and carried his gloom around like a cloud. Every "Bah! Humbug" that he muttered in the face of well-wishers and family members oozed bitterness. Someone once said, "Hate is like acid. It destroys the vessel that holds it." Hatred was destroying old Scrooge. Yet hate wasn't the end of his story. Through a well-known series of events that brought Scrooge face-to-face with his own choices, disappointments, and destiny, the miserable old man learned sorrow and repentance, and through repentance, joy. The changed Scrooge laughed out loud, shared his wealth freely, and capered like a schoolboy. He became a man transformed.

Another Christmas tale illustrates the wonder of transformation (that we seem more willing to believe in at Christmastime). Frank Capra's film *It's a Wonderful Life* tells of the metamorphosis of businessman and father George Bailey.[4] Business was going well at the Bailey Brothers Building and Loan Association until Uncle Billy lost the day's deposit. George's company and reputation, built through long years at the expense of great dreams, slipped through his fingers in a matter of moments. Helpless, George erupted into rage, hurling objects and shouting at the people he loved most. Ashamed and desperate, he drove recklessly to the town bar in an attempt to drown his pain. On a bar stool, in desperation, he whispered, "Dear Father, I'm not a praying man, but if you're up there and you can hear me, show me the way. I'm at the end of my rope. Show me the way, God."

George's troubles only became worse, and he concluded that God didn't hear his plea. Teetering on the railing of a bridge, facing the rushing waters below, George decided to end his hurt. Yet all the while, God had heard, and He was lovingly drawing George to Himself through his suffering. That night George saw and felt many things, each worse than the last. And like Scrooge, his choices and his destiny were shown to him. But through God's intervention George realized both how blessed he was and how needed and loved. He came home a new man, broken and grateful.

When I Am Weak

Far more powerful than the fictitious tales of Ebenezer Scrooge and George Bailey, the pages of Scripture reveal one of the most dramatic true transformations in Christian history. This transformation began on the road to the Syrian city of Damascus (Acts 9:1-31; 22:1-21; 26:1-18). Saul of Tarsus was traveling that road on a mission. By his own acknowledgment, before He met Jesus, he was a paragon of self-confidence. "If anyone else thinks he has reasons to put confidence in the flesh," he wrote in Philippians 3:4-6, "I have more: circumcised on the eighth day, of the people of Israel, of the tribe of Benjamin, a Hebrew of Hebrews; in regard to the law, a Pharisee; as for zeal, persecuting the church; as for legalistic righteousness, faultless."

Privileged in every way, he passionately followed every letter of the rigid teachings of the Pharisees. He had it all and was proud of it!

And Saul was a man who hated Christians (Acts 9:1). Incensed by the authority with which Jesus turned the Jewish Law on its head, Saul set out to eradicate the fledgling faith Jesus had sparked. He stood front and center at the murder of Stephen, Christianity's first martyr, holding cloaks and cheering on the killers. After instigating the massive persecution of Christians in Jerusalem, Saul traveled to Damascus with legal documents in hand, to track down and destroy more Christ-followers. Yet, as he approached the city, God derailed his plans. He was knocked off his high horse and his life was changed forever.

> Meanwhile, Saul was still breathing out murderous threats against the Lord's disciples. He went to the high priest and asked him for letters to the synagogues in Damascus, so that if he found any there who belonged to the Way, whether men or women, he might take them as prisoners to Jerusalem. As he neared Damascus on his journey, suddenly a light from heaven flashed around him. He fell to the ground and heard a voice say to him, "Saul, Saul, why do you persecute me?"
>
> "Who are you, Lord?" Saul asked.
>
> "I am Jesus, whom you are persecuting," he replied. "Now get up and go into the city, and you will be told what you must do."
>
> The men traveling with Saul stood there speechless; they heard the sound but did not see anyone. Saul got up from the ground, but when he opened his eyes he could see nothing. So they led him by the hand into Damascus. (Acts 9:1-8)

Before Saul met Jesus on the road to Damascus, his self-image was built on his personal pedigree and peerless performance. As Paul grew to know the Lord, his internal priorities were radically rearranged. Knowing Jesus and bringing others to know and love Him became Paul's driving passions. Deprivation, shipwrecks, repeated beatings, imprisonment, stonings, and exposure to the elements (2 Corinthians 11:23-29) served only to bring him closer to God. In fact, he came to embrace, rather than merely endure, weaknesses (2 Corinthians 12:7-10).

More Than Surviving

God wants every hurting and hurtful person to be transformed. Perhaps not the same way as Paul was, but changed, nonetheless.

The term *survivor* is a common designation for those who have experienced trauma. The word signifies someone who comes through hard times and doesn't give up. Yet, being a survivor does not seem to capture adequately what happened in the fictional lives of Ebenezer Scrooge and George Bailey, or in the lives of Paul, Zacchaeus, the Samaritan woman at the well, Matthew the former tax collector, the apostle Peter, and so many others. People were never meant to just get by or to grit their teeth and hang on by their fingernails. Yet the tragic reality is that we often settle for merely making it. Gordon MacDonald explained, "I have often smiled at the comment made by my friend who said, 'I started life thinking I'd hit a home run every time I came to bat. Now I just want to get through the game without getting beaned on the head by the ball.'"[5]

True life-change is vastly more than not being beaned on the head in the game of life.

When Jesus spoke of His mission on earth, He meant more than simply getting by. "He has sent me to proclaim freedom for the prisoners and recovery of sight for the blind, to release the oppressed" (Luke 4:18b). Jesus held an invincible beacon of hope for people living with pain, disillusionment, and despair.

More Than Justice

We have worked with many folks who have faced heart-rending trauma in their lives. A burning issue for most is to find the reason for the suffering. Perpetrators of abuse are easily identifiable, but with much of the pain we experience, we aren't able get our hands on the reason for it. Too often, there are no tidy explanations.

John chapter 9 tells us of a day when Jesus and His disciples saw a man who had been blind from birth. Jesus' disciples asked who was responsible for the man's blindness—he or his parents? The disciples had bought into the blame-game. They reasoned that somebody must have done something wrong in order for this man to suffer. Jesus, however, explained that it was neither this man's fault nor his parents'. Rather, "This happened so that the work of God might be displayed in his life" (John 9:3). There was no sin, no wrong to right, and no blame to place.

Justice on this earth is rarely the relief we hope it will be. True transformation does not require justice on this earth. Scrooge never recovered the Christmas vacations of his boyhood, when he was left alone and friendless at school while the other children rejoined loving families. Despicable Mr. Potter never returned George Bailey's hard-earned money. Though Saul repented, Stephen was not brought back to life. Yet all these men discovered new life and boundless joy.

True transformation is not simply coping, getting by, or putting up with the pain. Rather, redemptive suffering means the sexual abuse by your uncle, the betrayal by your spouse, the dishonesty of your Christian boss, or the rejection by your lover—the very events that have caused great anguish in your life—are faced and felt, but are now used for God's glory.

William Barclay, Scottish theologian and writer, explains, "endurance is not just the ability to bear a hard thing, but to turn it into glory."[6] Transformation means that the very thing with which the enemy meant to destroy you is now being used as a testimony of God's amazing work in your life. The past does not disappear, but it is seen from a different light.

God's Greatest Work: Tammy's Story

When I was about nine, a custodian in my elementary school regularly doled out handfuls of candy to kids in the halls and on the playgrounds. Wheat-germ, powdered skim milk, and other health food concoctions were the staples in my household, so anything sweet put a sparkle in my eyes and a craving in my stomach. One afternoon, I met Patrick in the hall and he slipped me more candies. This time, however, he whispered that I should come to the school on Saturday and he would give me lots of candies. He cautioned that I shouldn't tell anyone, because this was our secret. Otherwise, all the kids would want to come.

Saturday came and I asked to play outside; but instead, I furtively made my way to the school doors and Patrick let me in. He quickly led me to a classroom and I wondered where the candies were. There was no sweet food that day. Instead, this large man molested me.

I told no one that day or for years to come. I didn't want to say the words out loud. Years later, as I began counseling people, many came sharing stories of abuse. I realized that I needed to face what had happened to me. It took time for me to speak the words out loud, to face the truth, to look at ways I had hurt others through my self-protection, and to forgive. I continue to face my self-protective heart.

But that isn't the end of the story. In time, I began counseling more abused individuals, leading sexual abuse groups, conducting research on abuse, and speaking at sexual abuse conferences. The first class I taught at Providence Seminary was Counseling the Abused. Ironic? No. Paradoxically, *the place where we have been broken the most is often the place where God wants to do His greatest work.* The most helpless places are where He wants to be our strength. The abuse was a chapter in my life story. However, it was not the conclusion or even the theme. This event, and others that God has sovereignly permitted, have influenced my way of seeing life and my way of relating to others. When people read or hear my story, I pray they see that God is bigger than the abuse. I pray that others will want to know about the God who is transforming me. "This happened so that the work of God might be displayed in [my] life" (John 9:3).

In the civilian uprisings in Paris during the early 1800s, insurrectionists built barricades across the Parisian streets and fought from behind wagons, carts, broken beams, and any other object they could pile between themselves and their opponents. Less well-equipped than the soldiers of the ruling French government, the insurrectionists soon ran short of bullets, and they restocked by raiding the fallen bodies of soldiers on the other side of the barricades. They then used this ammunition to defeat their enemies. God's plan is similar. We are designed to take the ammunition the enemy has hurled at us in an attempt to destroy us, and use it against him. Real transformation involves taking the verbal, physical, and sexual bullets of the enemy and instead of hurting and hating others in response, allowing God to redeem what has been broken. Our worst wounds become His greatest tools.

Whose Job Is it to Change People Anyway?

Who, then, is the initiator in this healing? Who teaches us to turn the ammunition of the enemy back on him? Whose job is it to change people anyway?

When George Bailey stormed out of his home in a rage, Peter Bailey asked his mom, "Is Daddy in trouble?" Mary Bailey anxiously answered yes. Tiny Janie Bailey piped up, "Shall I pray for him?" And her mom answered wisely, "Yes Janie, pray very hard."

God is the designer and initiator of the process of life-change. He loves it when His people call on Him on behalf of others. *It's a Wonderful Life* is a fictional story, but there are sound principles to be gleaned. When George Bailey, broken and humbled, called out to God, "Please God, let me live again!" the movie showed that God heard. It was what God had wanted for George all along. George's family, though they loved him, could not solve his problem, and they could not heal his anguish.

What, then, can *we* do? Like Janie, caregivers need to "pray very hard" for the transformation of the people we serve. When Jesus faced the cross, what did He do? "He fell with His face to the ground and prayed..." (Matthew 26:39). At His most difficult hour, He talked with His Father. We cannot redeem people ourselves. Our prayers, however, do not go unheard; when we pray, God is not *compelled* to act, but He is *moved* to act, because He loves us and the people for whom we are praying. Imagine what would happen if we loved people enough to fall with our faces to the ground and pray for their transformation.

We cannot take responsibility for choices made by the people we counsel. We can direct, guide, love, empathize, and pray for them; but with all this care, some choose to follow God, and others choose to turn away from Him. The reality is that no matter the source or severity of our pain, one man, in his anguish, meets God and is transformed, while another chooses to give up on God forever.

YetYou Have Not Returned to Me...

The Prophet Amos described a time in Israel's history when the people ignored the rebuke of God and refused His transforming touch, despite great cost to themselves:

> "I gave you empty stomachs in every city and lack of bread in every town, *yet you have not returned to me*," declares the LORD. "I also withheld rain from you when the harvest was still three months away. I sent rain on one town, but withheld it from another. One field had rain; another had none and dried up. People staggered from town to town for water but did not get enough to drink, *yet you have not returned to me*," declares the LORD. "Many times I struck your gardens and vineyards, I struck them with blight and mildew. Locusts devoured your fig and olive trees, *yet you have not returned to me*," declares the LORD. "I sent plagues among you as I did to Egypt. I killed

your young men with the sword, along with your
captured horses. I filled your nostrils with the stench
of your camps, *yet you have not returned to me,*" declares
the LORD. "I overthrew some of you as I overthrew
Sodom and Gomorrah. You were like a burning
stick snatched from the fire, *yet you have not returned to
me,*" declares the LORD. "Therefore this is what I will
do to you, Israel, and because I will do this to you,
prepare to meet your God, O Israel." (Amos 4:6-12,
emphasis added)

Many times in Israel's history, God brought His people back to
Himself through suffering. He did not relish the pain they suffered;
but it was far better than letting them throw away the blessing they
had of being His people. Yet Amos says that this time, Israel did
not hear. God would not force them to a decision. He called and
invited them, showed them how frail their well-being could be, and
reminded them of His past faithfulness to them; but He let them
choose. Amos, his prophet, urged and rebuked Israel in God's name,
but he could not force them to change. It was not his task.

God's Means of Life-Change

The book of Amos is a portion of God's perfect Word where He
made it unmistakably obvious that people devoid of His Word wither
and decay. "My people are destroyed from a lack of knowledge"
(Hosea 4:6). Conversely, absorbing Scripture has often resulted in
life-change.

In his book, *Reflections on the Movies,*[7] Ken Gire discusses the movie,
Amistad.[8] The movie chronicles the tortuous journey made by fifty-
three enslaved Africans who were brutally beaten, many killed. The
slaves were transported by a Cuban ship, the *Amistad.* The goal of the
captors was to deliver the human "property" to a plantation in the
Caribbean. However, the African slaves took over their captors' ship

and killed some of the crew with the intent of sailing back to Africa. An American ship then seized the *Amistad* and brought the slaves to the U.S. where they were charged with murder. On March 9, 1841, the case went to the Supreme Court in *United States v the Amistad*.

Awaiting their verdict in an over-crowded prison, Jamba, one of the prisoners, studied a Bible that was given to him by a Christian abolitionist. He couldn't read the English words but he was able to understand the story of Jesus through the picture Bible.

Cinque, the leader of the revolt, observed Jamba closely and, full of suspicion, muttered, "You don't have to pretend to be interested in that. Nobody's watching but me."

Jamba replied, "I'm not pretending. I'm beginning to understand it."

Then, Jamba proceeded to show the pictures of Jesus' life, death, and resurrection and tell His story. The two men talked about the suffering Jesus faced and they concluded that this innocent man understood pain and His captors weren't able to destroy Him.

Jamba explained, "They thought He was dead but He appeared before His people again…and spoke to them. Then, finally, He rose into the sky."

Cinque responded, "This is just a story, Jamba."

But Jamba disagreed.

In a dark cell, a prisoner awaiting possible death is set emotionally and spiritually free through reading a picture Bible.

God's Word has the power to set captives free whether the shackles are made of alcohol, food, pornography, or steel.

One of the most neglected teachings of Scripture about transformation is the work of God's Holy Spirit. A man named Tim embodies this biblical teaching in an amazing way. His life was adrift. He was loaded with mountains of anger and he seethed with pride and self-confidence. He says he was a self-centered pleasure-seeker. Others agree. He and I (Roger) began meeting weekly in late September, but he kept me at arm's length. In a January meeting with him I mentioned my upcoming annual teaching trip to Germany over spring break. "Is there a chance I could go with you?" he asked.

"If you can find a ticket" was my reply. He found one about $100 cheaper than mine!

By the end of the first week in Germany he had been in lots of prayer meetings, heard hours and hours of teaching, and seen hundreds of people. His mind was swirling with new images of German culture, but also of his painful (and quite sinful) past. The day of teaching had been long and as midnight approached, I was ready for bed. Tim cautiously raised a question about his sinful history. "Tim, you have no idea how much God loves you, anyway, junk and all!" I told him. That triggered another hour of talking, weeping, and praying together. God lifted the oppressive weight of sin and guilt from his broken, shame-filled heart.

God's Holy Spirit began a life-transformation in this young man that has been astounding to observe. Christlike servanthood, kindness, integrity, and humility began to mark his speech and actions. A new and exciting vision for his future, now under God's direction, started to take shape in our conversations. Back on campus, everyone who had known him before the trip was amazed at what God was doing. The body was the same, but the person inside that athlete's frame was being radically made-new by the supernatural work of the Holy Spirit. In the two years since the trip, God has also brought a lovely Christian woman into his life. Tim often tells others how God has been changing him, encouraging them to experience His transforming work as well.

Transformed by the Holy Spirit

As believers are filled with and *controlled* by the Holy Spirit, they develop God's internal power to forgive, to be kind to enemies, to overcome temptation, and to be thankful for growth through painful experiences. Scars remain, to be sure, yet they do not defeat us, and they do not embitter us; God's character shines through.

A look into Canadian winters may help illustrate this truth. I (Tammy) grew up in "Winterpeg, Manicolda" as I affectionately refer to my homeland, Canada's often harsh Mid-west. Manitobans are hardy folks who endure bitterly cold winters. During these icy months as temperatures plunge ever lower, we hear the weather channels announce the diminishing number of seconds that skin can be exposed without freezing!

We frequently spend our mornings shoveling driveways so our cars can exit. Shoveling requires gloves. Yet, it is obvious that gloves, alone, cannot move a single snowflake. Gloves, though powerless by themselves, were formed to be filled with powerful hands. Christ's Spirit is the all-powerful hand of God who fills and enables our spiritually powerless lives to accomplish everything God wants of us (Philippians 4:13). His indwelling presence produces eternal changes in us, empowering us to do things uniquely suited to His purposes for our lives.

> The Spirit filled a boy who played upon a harp and made him a psalmist (1 Samuel 16:18), a shepherd and herdsman who pruned sycamore trees and made him a prophet (Amos 7:14-15), a boy given to abstinence (Daniel 1:8) and made him a judge of mature men, a fisherman and made him a preacher (Matthew 4:19), a persecutor and made him the teacher of Gentiles (Acts 9:1-20), a tax collector and made him an evangelist (Luke 5:27-28). What a skillful workman this Spirit is! The Spirit's very touch is teaching. It changes a human mind in a moment to enlighten it; suddenly what it was it no longer is, suddenly it is what it was not. (Gregory the Great, c. 540-604) as quoted in Burgess[9]

Catastrophe, pain, loss, and rejection do not change people by themselves. Some people respond to pain with bitterness, passivity, self-righteousness, or a life of addiction. Instead, God intends adversity to bring us back to Him in order to redeem us, so His Holy Spirit can make us new. And what is the responsibility of the Christian caregiver? To "keep in step with the Spirit" (Galatians 5:25) and pray for others to do the same.

Keeping in step with God's Spirit is simply doing what God wants us to do, as revealed in His perfect Word. It is hearing the story He is telling and playing our role in it; it is understanding the quest He is on and being a part of it. God, Himself, brings about the changes. And the changes He makes leave us full of joy, full of tenderness, and full of beauty. He gives us, as Isaiah 61:3 tells, "a crown of beauty instead of ashes, the oil of gladness instead of mourning, and a garment of praise instead of a spirit of despair"!

Reflections

1. To look more like Jesus, we often must allow God to do a *Clean Sweep* in our lives. What is some of "the stuff" in your life that He is asking you to get rid of?

2. Ponder the words, *the place where we have been broken the most is often the place where God wants to do His greatest* work. What are the broken places in your life He wants to redeem?

3. In your own words, what does it mean to be transformed?

4. What would it mean if you really embraced the fact that true transformation comes from God and not ourselves? How could this truth transform your caregiving?

Notes

[1] Klein, M. (Producer). *What Not to Wear* [Television series episode] (New York: Discovery Communications Inc.), 2003.

[2] French, K. et al. (Producers). *Clean Sweep* [Television series episode] (New York: Discovery Communications Inc.), 2003.

[3] Jones, John Daniel. "The Optimism of Jesus" in W. W. Wiersbe (Ed.), *Classic Sermons on Hope* (Grand Rapids: Kregel Publications), 1994, p. 29.

[4] Stern, P. V. D. et. al. (Writers); Capra, Frank (Producer/Director). *It's a Wonderful Life* [Motion picture] (Hollywood: Universal Studios Home Video), 1946.

[5] MacDonald, Gordon. *Mid-course Correction* (Nashville: Thomas Nelson, Inc.), 2000, p. xi.

[6] William Barclay, 1907-1978, Scottish theologian, religious writer, broadcaster. Quote is often attributed to him but without documentation (www.borntomotivate.com).

[7] Gire, Ken. *Reflections on the Movies.* (Colorado Springs: Victor), 2003, pp. 175-178.

[8] Spielberg, Steven et al. (Producers). *Amistad* [Motion picture] (Universal City: DreamWorks Pictures), 1997.

[9] Burgess, Stanley M. *The Holy Spirit: Medieval Roman Catholic and Reformation Traditions* (Peabody Mass.: Hendrickson Publishers, Inc.), 1997.

CHAPTER NINE

When the Journey Is Too Much

How Can Christian Caregivers Deal With Burnout?

O Lord, how long will you forget me? Forever? How long will you look the other way? How long must I struggle with anguish in my soul, with sorrow in my heart every day? – Psalm 13:1-2

The Malady of the Ministry: Tammy's Story

During my doctoral studies, my apartment stood adjacent to a neighbor's back yard. The yard was a wilderness of discarded furniture, rusting car parts, and empty beer bottles. In the corner of the yard stood a cage overgrown with weeds; in the cage sat a rickety dog house, piles of animal feces, and an old beagle. She was a pitiful beagle, over-fed and under-loved. Most evenings I would put my hand through the cage and pat the broken-down old dog, and

Dixie would wag her tail and howl with delight as beagles do. Over the years Dixie's owners had shown little love for their pet. She was discarded, like a bottle of beer already drunk. I ached when I passed by old Dixie-dog.

A caregiver friend recently e-mailed me the following message: "Please pray. I am burnt out, discouraged, I want to quit."

I understood those words. Burnout is endemic to the caregiving profession. It is the malady of this ministry. After long days of tedious sessions with no breakthroughs despite all our education, experience, and efforts, we find ourselves feeling less like torch-bearers and more like old beagles. We come to share a kindred spirit with used-up, forgotten Dixie, and we express it with words like "I am burnt out…I want to quit." We understand the sense of being broken down and depleted, locked in a cage of other people's sorrow, hoping someone might come along and extend a friendly hand.

A Gnawing Theme

Being the confidant to the anguish and impiety of people hour after hour evokes a unique stress in caregivers. There are pressures and heartaches that are inevitable in the caregiving field, pressures that can drain and crush helpers from the inside and from the outside. Caregivers take hurting people's "anguish to bed with them at night and grieve about it in their dreams; it remains like a gnawing theme in the back of their minds" (Chessick as quoted in Mahoney).[1]

As we stand by those trying to understand their feelings and regain their joy, ironically we often find that our own thoughts and feelings prey upon us. In our experiences with caregivers (and with our own times of burnout), we have found that the hardest times to go on are when we are feeling futile, alone, and overwhelmed. These feelings arise out of the unavoidable difficulties of the practice of caregiving, and if not dealt with, they lay waste to the efforts and good intentions of even the most compassionate caregivers.

Futility saps our strength and makes our small victories and our big sacrifices ring hollow. Caregivers develop a colossal sorrow from hearing of all this suffering, injustice, and evil, and we can begin to feel powerless against the magnitude of human need. We feel robbed of the opportunity to actually help hurting people because there are always more hurting people to help—many more. One study of the sources of stress for therapists revealed that the "lack of therapeutic success" is the single most stressful aspect of the career.[2]

It is easy for caregivers to feel alone. We may not have developed a team of people to support us as we listen to the heartbreaking stories that our clients entrust to us. Issues of confidentiality bar us from sharing the load by talking about what we've heard. While our hearts are breaking for the people we sit with, the world goes on without caring or even noticing our clients' pain or ours. At times, we watch clients we have grown to care for, make foolish decisions. On many days, caregiving is disappointing and lonely.

The result of laboring alone is usually laboring too much. Overwork is a specter most caregivers will deal with at some point in their calling. The relentless list of appointments, deadlines, calls to return, and staff meetings to endure leaves us no time for recovery. In mental health centers we carry schedules that are overloaded with distressed people in order to meet *productivity* (the number of clients mental health centers determine counselors must see in a given month). Many caregivers stagger under the weight of the never-ending paperwork. Then there are pastors with several emergency counseling situations that strike the same week as a wedding, funeral, and the Sunday sermon preparation. Missionaries, teachers, youth workers, parents—all juggle their own needs, the needs of those they care for, and the everyday requirements of living. And as a result they have no time left to recover from their labor. Caregivers become trapped and smothered from the weight of people to sit with and tasks to complete.

As out-of-balance car tires irritate and endanger travel, the imbalance of our lives irritates us and endangers our effectiveness in relationships. We are like a candle burning at both ends—creating twice the light but vanishing in half the time. Like abused women stuck in the cycle of violence, we become stuck in the cycle of our overwork, over-responsibility, and over-exhaustion.

Is there hope for us? Does God care about our wounds and our weariness, or is He as disappointed in us as we are? As we have often found, God's Word is a healing balm to the crispy-fried caregiver. We find understanding in the pages of Scripture, where we read of great men and women of God who often have experienced the same hurts and failings, and offer to share their hope.

Under the Broom Tree: Feeling Futile

Elijah, the man of God, the miracle-worker, the mighty prophet who never tasted death: he is one of the most revered servants of God in the Old Testament. He was a great prophet and praying man in a depraved period of Israel's history. When we find him in 1 Kings 18, he is challenging 450 priests of the false god Baal and, at God's instruction, calling down fire from Heaven. Yet chapter 19 opens with the prophet on the run and in despair:

> Now Ahab told Jezebel everything Elijah had done and how he had killed all the prophets with the sword. So Jezebel sent a messenger to Elijah to say: "May the gods deal with me, be it ever so severely, if by this time tomorrow I do not make your life like that of one of them." Elijah was afraid and ran for his life. When he came to Beersheba in Judah, he left his servant there while he himself went a day's journey into the desert. He came to a broom tree, sat down under it and prayed that he might die. "I have had enough, LORD," he said. "Take my life; I am no better than my ancestors." Then he lay down under the tree and fell asleep. (1 Kings 19:2-5)

Elijah wanted out. He wanted to die. And we ask, "What brought one of the greatest prophets of God to such a point?"

On the day he fled to the desert, Elijah had been used to defeat the 450 priests of Baal. At Mount Carmel Elijah had challenged the priests and the people of Israel to choose whom they would serve, God or Baal. Setting out a prepared sacrifice, the priests called upon Baal to ignite the sacrifice and demonstrate his power. From morning until evening the priests cried out to Baal. In desperation they took knives and cut themselves in hope that the smell of blood would attract their bloodthirsty god. He answered with silence.

Then Elijah soaked the wood and the remaining bull so thoroughly with water that a surrounding trench was filled to the brim. He uttered a humble prayer, asking God to answer:

> "O Lord, God of Abraham, Isaac and Israel, let it be known today that you are God in Israel and that I am your servant and have done all these things at your command. Answer me, O LORD, answer me, so these people will know that you, O LORD, are God, and that you are turning their hearts back again." (1 Kings 18:36-37)

God responded with an inferno that roared down from heaven, burning up the sacrifice, wood, stones, water, and all, and reclaiming Israel as His own. The false prophets of Baal were executed by the people. Elijah prayed for rain and God sent it after a three-and-a-half-year drought. Then Elijah was supernaturally empowered to run ahead of Ahab's chariot on a muddy, rain-soaked road fifteen miles to Jezreel (1 Kings 18:40-46). These were spectacular answers to prayer, all in one day!

Yet, the next day Elijah's spiritual high crashed. When Queen Jezebel, who had replaced the nation's true prophets with prophets of Baal, heard what Elijah had done to her servants, she swore vengeance. She had already murdered all of his counterparts, and Elijah knew she did not speak in vain. He ran for the hills.

Alone in the wilderness, Elijah collapsed under a broom tree, burnt out, despondent, and wanting to die. "I have had enough, Lord," he said. "Take my life; I am no better than my ancestors" (1 Kings 19:4). After all he had done, and all that God had done through him, Elijah felt "no better than [his] ancestors," no different from the prophets who had served and died and still left Israel to the likes of King Ahab and Queen Jezebel. All had been for nothing.

I Am the Only One Left: Feeling Alone

Elijah's despair was not solely because he felt futile. He was haunted by a feeling that wreaks havoc on the human soul: the feeling of being utterly alone.

> ...And after the fire came a gentle whisper. When Elijah heard it, he pulled his cloak over his face and went out and stood at the mouth of the cave. Then a voice said to him, "What are you doing here, Elijah?" He replied, "I have been very zealous for the LORD God Almighty. The Israelites have rejected your covenant, broken down your altars, and put your prophets to death with the sword. I am the only one left, and now they are trying to kill me too." (1 Kings 19:12-14)

I am the only one left. What a desolate, desperate phrase—to believe you are the only survivor of a mass execution, a nationwide martyrdom of God's prophets in God's own nation. And now they were after him, too. How could one man stand against such brutality? Who could Elijah turn to, now that he assumed all had turned to Baal, or died refusing?

A Still Small Voice: Restoring Purpose and Companionship

Where was God at the point of Elijah's desperation? The same place He is for all of His worn-out caregivers—waiting, with arms open wide. God, the best of all caregivers, saw Elijah's despair and cared for him. He knew that the desert was no place to reprimand Elijah for weakness or for lack of faith. Instead, He provided a place for Elijah to sleep under the broom tree. He prepared breakfast to restore his energy reserves, and then let him sleep some more (19:5-6). The Angel of the Lord awakened him with a touch. He encouraged Elijah to talk honestly about his grief (19:9-14). He gave him time to get away and process what had happened to him. Before God called Elijah to move on to the next task, He compassionately said to His servant, "the journey is too much for you" and so He gave Elijah more food and drink (Spurgeon as quoted by Exell).[3]

God's gentle heart knew exactly what His beloved servant needed. He knows when the journey is too much for us. And He will restore us. When we are burnt out and running from the Jezebels in our lives, God pursues us and has a broom tree waiting. "As the hound follows the hare, never ceasing in its running, ever drawing to the chase...so does God follow the fleeing soul by his Divine grace."[4]

When Elijah's strength had been restored, God let him know that he had more to do. His life had purpose. Despite Elijah's failure, God did not hate him. God was not sick of him. God would not throw him away. Elijah was called to anoint others to carry on His work (1 Kings 19:15-16).

And God told Elijah that he was not alone. There were 7,000 others in Israel who had not bowed their knees to Baal (19:18). He was not the only one remaining faithful, and he did not have to carry on with the task alone.

Elijah had lost perspective that day. In his state of mind, the threat of one wicked woman suddenly loomed larger than 450 false prophets. So often we caregivers lose perspective when we have a gigantic stack of reports waiting on our desks, numerous phone calls to return, and several more desperate people to see today. Elijah lost his grand view of the almighty God who hears and answers prayer. Under the broom trees of our lives, God invites us to call on Him. We pray for many reasons. But when we are depleted, worn out, fed up, and burnt out, we realize that prayer is also "… a cry from the bare spot in our lives, from the empty space, from the part of us that is missing. It is the wounded part seeking to be healed, the missing part seeking to be found, the now-dry clay of the sculpture seeking the hands that first touched it, first caressed it, first loved it."[5]

Under the broom trees of our lives, He hears our groans and He cares.

> The Israelites groaned in their slavery and cried out, and their cry for help because of their slavery went up to God. God heard their groaning and He remembered His covenant with Abraham, with Isaac and with Jacob. *So God looked on the Israelites and was concerned about them.* (Exodus 2:23-25, emphasis added).

And He is concerned about His caregivers!

From Morning Till Evening: Feeling Overwhelmed

Moses, another great hero of faith from the Old Testament, had reason to feel overwhelmed. The people of Israel were an unruly, ungrateful nation at best, even as they witnessed miracle after miracle in the desert after God had set them free from Egypt. The emancipation of the people from Pharaoh's grasp was not the culmination of Moses' work, but the beginning. For the next forty years, Moses faithfully and compassionately guided, advocated for, and judged among the people God had given him to lead.

Moses thought the endless work was all his to bear. His father-in-law, observing long lines of people waiting the whole day to get to Moses for decisions about their affairs, had a different opinion:

> The next day Moses took his seat to serve as judge for the people, and they stood around him from morning till evening. When his father-in-law saw all that Moses was doing for the people, he said, "What is

this you are doing for the people? Why do you alone sit as judge, while all these people stand around you from morning till evening?" Moses answered him, "Because the people come to me to seek God's will. Whenever they have a dispute, it is brought to me, and I decide between the parties and inform them of God's decrees and laws." (Exodus 18:13-16)

Jethro discerned that Moses had not learned to delegate lesser issues to those around him, and he told his son-in-law:

"What you are doing is not good. You and these people who come to you will only wear yourselves out. The work is too heavy for you; you cannot handle it alone. Listen now to me and I will give you some advice, and may God be with you. You must be the people's representative before God and bring their disputes to him. Teach them the decrees and laws, and show them the way to live and the duties they are to perform. But select capable men from all the people—men who fear God, trustworthy men who hate dishonest gain—and appoint them as officials over thousands, hundreds, fifties and tens. Have them serve as judges for the people at all times, but have them bring every difficult case to you; the simple cases they can decide themselves. That will make your load lighter, because they will share it with you. If you do this and God so commands, you will be able to stand the strain, and all these people will go home satisfied." (Exodus 18:17-23)

Moses trusted his father-in-law and took his advice. He ceased believing the work was his sole responsibility and he began delegating to others.

Overwork is a common root of burnout. Most caregivers are acutely aware of what it means to work too many hours. There is always one more person in need of help, always one more phone call to make, always one more report to write up, always one more hospital visit. When we are weary and discouraged, God lovingly imparts these words: *"The work is too heavy for you; you cannot handle it alone."*

Many Christian caregivers work in a context where external paperwork and productivity demands cannot be delegated or lessened. In those times we must find other ways to have our peace restored, as we will discuss in the next section. Yet some of our busyness is our own doing. My (Tammy's) thesis for my master's degree centered on reasons why many caregivers enter the helping profession and ministry. I discovered that many of us, as kids, couldn't make our depressed dad feel better, stop our sister from drinking so much, or help our mom and dad get back together. Thus, we embark on helping careers to fix in others what we couldn't fix in our own families.

When we do this, we don't help out of freedom, but out of our desire to minimize our helplessness. We become fixers. And when the people we are trying to help don't change, and others around us aren't working as hard as we are, we become irritated with them and sometimes with God. Like Martha we complain to God, "Don't you care that my sister has left me to do the work by myself? Tell her to help me!" (Luke 10:40). We may say this directly to God, or we may express it through our fury with other people and with our circumstances. Either way, we forget that God directs our circumstances, and that griping at people and the way things are going is much like grumbling about God, and leads to the same bitterness of heart. We can't make people get better. We can't heal all the evil in this world. And instead of realizing that this was never designed to be our job, we become frustrated, angry, and burnt out.

To Lonely Places: Restoring Peace

Jesus loved those around Him. He sacrificed and gave of Himself again and again, out of a pure and intense love. Yet He kept a proper perspective of His work. Jesus was a perfectly balanced model and He chose to live within the limitations of human existence. He was not driven to cure everyone around Him. He realized the poor would always be with us (Matthew 26:11). In John 17:4 Jesus makes this astonishing statement in prayer to His Father, "I have brought you glory on earth by completing the work you gave me to do." How could Jesus possibly say He had completed the work God gave Him to do? There were still so many leprous, lame, blind, and sinful people desperate for His hands! But Jesus' task was not to bind up all wounds or cure all illnesses. It was to help people learn to love Him, honor Him, and worship Him—and thus to find new life.

In the midst of His healing and teaching, Jesus repeatedly left the crowds and went away quietly to be with His Father. Matthew 14:23 tells us that "After he had dismissed them, he went up on a mountainside by himself to pray..." and Luke 5:16 recounts, "But Jesus often withdrew to lonely places and prayed."

The aches among those around us are too much for us to handle alone. We were designed to come away from the crowd, to turn off the television and close the door, to become quiet and to sit with our Father and be renewed. Richard Foster said it well,

> Jesus calls us from loneliness to solitude. The fear of being left alone petrifies people... Our fear of being alone drives us to noise and crowds. We keep up a constant stream of words even if they are inane [foolish]. We buy radios that strap to our wrists or fit over our ears so that, if no one else is around, at least we are not condemned to silence.[6]

The Dark Night of the Soul...and the Dawn

Foster also explains,

> To take seriously the discipline of solitude will mean that at some point or points along the pilgrimage we will enter what St. John of the

Cross vividly describes as "the dark night of the soul." The "dark night" to which he calls us is not something bad or destructive. On the contrary, it is an experience to be welcomed much as a sick person might welcome a surgery that promises health and well being. The purpose of the darkness is not to punish or to afflict us. It is to set us free. St. John of the Cross embraced the soul's dark night as a divine appointment, a privileged opportunity to draw close to the divine Center…The dark night is one of the ways God brings us into a hush, a stillness so that he may work an inner transformation upon the soul.[7]

Roger remembers: In 1980, I went through four months of bleak and lonely depression, the "dark night" of which Foster wrote. I felt a profound sense of failure as a leader and as a man. Through a leadership nightmare, maligning comments were made, precious friends walked away, and deep sorrow and loneliness engulfed me. In the midst of my depression, I learned that the surgical and renewing power of God's truth in the Bible was effective in filling my thinking with God Himself, displacing the defeat and despair. I repeatedly saw that my puny human strength is so majestically dwarfed by God's unlimited power and wisdom that total trust in God is the only logical response. Oh, how I wish I would learn to live in perpetual rest in the stillness with Jesus! But over time a few moments of rest have grown into seasons. Those restful seasons with the Lord prompt this passionate invitation: Weary reader, rush to His throne of grace and be renewed, "finding as He promised, perfect peace and rest."[8]

He is not a God who uses us and throws us away when we break. He is not a God who forgets His servants and friends. He is a God who cares for us while we care for others; who heals us when we feel futile, alone, overwhelmed, and burnt out. "Therefore, since through God's mercy we have this ministry, we do not lose heart… We are hard pressed on every side, but not crushed; perplexed, but not in despair; persecuted, but not abandoned; struck down, but not destroyed" (2 Corinthians 4:1, 8-9).

Our prayer for you, our brothers and sisters, is that in the midst of your pain and your frustration, your fear and your doubt, that you would run to the desert; and that there you would find a broom tree, and a still small voice, and the God who renews your strength.

Reflections

1. Describe a time when you suffered burnout while seeking to help hurting people. Try to put words to the barrenness of your soul during that time.

2. How would you like the Lord to show you how much He cares for you in this desert place?

3. Ponder the thought that God will renew you. What are ways to keep living in this renewal in the future?

Notes

[1] Mahoney, Michael J. *Human Change Processes* (New York: Basic Books, Inc.), 1991, p. 357.

[2] Farber, B. A, & Heifetz, L. J. "The Process and Dimension of Burnout in Psychotherapists," *Professional Psychology*, 1982, 13, 293-301.

[3] Exell, Joseph S. *The Biblical Illustrator, Volume 4 - I & II Samuel, I & II Kings.* (Grand Rapids: Baker Book House), 1973 "I Kings," p. 239.

[4] Thompson, Francis. *The Hound of Heaven and Other Poems* (Boston: International Pocket Library), 1936.

[5] Gire, Ken. *Between Heaven and Earth* (New York: HarperCollins), 1997, p. 79.

[6] Foster, Richard J. *The Celebration of Discipline* (San Francisco: Harper & Row, Publishers), 1978, p. 84.

[7] Ibid., pp. 89-90.

[8] Havergal, Frances R. "Like a River Glorious," *The Hymnal for Worship & Celebration* (Waco, TX: Word), 1986, p. 494.

CHAPTER TEN

Come, Let Us Rebuild
The Journey of Prayer

Without God, we cannot; without us, God will not. – Augustine

The wonder is not that we pray so little, but that we can ever get up from our knees if we realize our own need. – Unknown Christian

For the grace of God that brings salvation has appeared to all men. It teaches us to say "No" to ungodliness and worldly passions, and to live self-controlled, upright and godly lives in this present age, while we wait for the blessed hope—the glorious appearing of our great God and Savior, Jesus Christ, who gave himself for us to redeem us from all wickedness and to purify for himself a people that are his very own, eager to do what is good. – Paul (Titus 2:11-14)

All Our Former Pleasures

He was a compulsive liar and a gambler who stole from his family and friends. He was fourteen years of age the night his mother lay dying, and he spent the night drinking and playing cards. George was a young man who lived entirely for himself. His father was a Prussian tax collector who stuffed George's wallet with wads of cash. During his late teens, George collected and pocketed taxes owed to his father by villagers. The stolen loot financed his stays in expensive hotels with plenty of women. Despite the cash in his pocket, he had a favorite ruse that involved spending a week in a luxurious hotel, then making a quick getaway without paying the bill.

George's deception finally caught up to him and he landed in jail. His wealthy father bailed him out after a month's time and tried to beat the wicked ways out of his son. But the beating didn't cure him.

At 19 years of age, George entered Halle University as a student of divinity, still up to his old tricks. Then something happened to one of his drinking buddies. His friend Beta started attending a Saturday evening gathering, a Bible study where people were different. Curious, George convinced his friend to take him. The people there were kind and welcoming. But there was something even more powerful than their warmth. When these folks talked to God, they knelt. George had never seen that kind of praying before. He felt awkward being in a room with people who talked to God like He was their friend. But as George walked home that evening, he acknowledged, "…all our former pleasures are as nothing in comparison with this evening."[1]

That Saturday evening, George Müller met Jesus and the restoration process began. Müller is now regarded as one of the mightiest men of prayer in history. Having given up his swindled money and with only fifty cents in his pocket, George made his needs known only to God—and then raised millions of dollars to build Ashley Downs in Bristol, England, an orphanage housing 1,200 children. Millions of dollars were raised without ever publicizing financial needs. Instead, George prayed to his great God who has "cattle on a thousand hills" (Psalm 50:10). He understood that God designed His world to be impacted through the intercession of His people. He continued interceding for the salvation of friends for more than 50 years, a paragon of earnest faith and ceaseless prayer.

George's journey did not begin with his divinity studies, or his jail time, or his father's beatings. It began with the relationship that George glimpsed in people who prayed as though God was their friend.

Isn't it interesting to note the kind of people God has chosen to use to do His great work? David, who had an eye for another man's wife. Saul, a pitiless Christian-killer. The promiscuous Samaritan woman. And George Müller, a man whose chief ambition was to eat, drink, and be merry. God didn't select the people with the most promising résumés. He chose individuals who had been broken and had life-changing encounters with Jesus. He chose people through relationship, so they would lead others to Him as they had been led.

A New Paradigm

We have sought to illuminate a new paradigm in Christian caregiving. It is simply this: Prayer and counseling are inseparable. Prayer is not peripheral to counseling. Truly aiding people in anguish is a bigger task than you or we can do. God never meant for us to carry the heavy load of people's pain by ourselves. Jesus said, "Without me you can do nothing" (John 15:5). Spiritually speaking, we can't give true life-changing help to anyone without God's power. Caregivers are designed to turn to God for help by praying for the hurting and hurtful people they walk with. And when we do that, we can enthusiastically say with Paul, "I can do everything through Him who gives me strength" (Philippians 4:13).

When caregivers, and the ones for whom they care, sincerely turn to God for help, transformation is the inevitable result. This does not always mean that our circumstances will change. But it does mean that we will change.

It is time now to start on the journey, time to turn to God, to close these pages, and to begin. It is time to accept the great gift that has been offered us—the gift of intimately conversing with God. This relationship brings with it all that we have longed for—healing, and joy, and peace. But greater even than these gifts is the connection with God, who is the gift we have really needed all along.

As we go, there are still many questions. What will this transformation look like in my own life? How do I start on the journey of prayer? How do I continue when all seems against me? How do I create a legacy of transformation through prayer, even when others' paths diverge from my own? We want to point you to God, who in His eagerness to be with you is running forward along the path to meet you. He will walk beside you along the entire journey.

Desiring the Journey of Prayer

By picking up this book, you have begun to take intentional steps toward God because He has awakened spiritual hunger within you. You may be in the thick of the ministry of counseling (formal or informal), and feeling inadequate or burnt out. Perhaps you are just starting in counseling, and you fear the lack of results and the burnout that you have seen in other caregivers. Perhaps this was to be the last stop before you gave up. But no matter where you are in your career as a caregiver, something is calling to you—something that says there has to be a better way. The *desire for a better way* has already been born in you.

That *better way*, we are certain, is a relationship with God—a loving partnership that fuels and fills your caregiving. The way we enter that relationship is through prayer. But how do we undertake the journey of becoming praying caregivers?

The streets are thronged with people in anguish. But their urgent need alone will not move us to pray. *Guilty* is the word many Christians use to describe how they feel about their prayer lives, wishing they spent more quality time conversing with God. Guilt, however, seldom inspires people to seek God earnestly. If it produces any change at all, the change usually disappears as soon as the guilt-enforcer leaves the room. We've never heard of anyone who became mighty in prayer because of self-contempt. Shame merely drives people to veil their passionless praying. We do not want your journey of prayer to be riddled with guilt.

Fear is a poor change agent, as well. A few will abandon their risky pursuits out of fear of the consequences, but not many. Addicts keep drinking, puffing, overworking, and pursuing their lusts despite medical warnings and family pleas that they are destroying themselves. Threatening people with the blessings they miss because they don't pray has moved only a small number to prevail in prayer. We do not want you to start out the door because of fear.

What then makes us become the people of prayer we were meant to be? We start the journey of becoming praying men and women for a variety of reasons. There are many factors that can drive us toward change.

Sometimes, pain pushes us to call out to Jesus. Pain can prompt us to be aware of our great need for God. Jim Cymbala, a pastor and author of the groundbreaking book Fresh Wind, Fresh Fire, had one of those earth-shattering aha! moments, when he was struck by the relationship between pain and prayer. "I discovered an astonishing truth: God is attracted to weakness. He can't resist those who humbly and honestly admit how desperately they need Him."[2] We always need Him. Pain reminds us of our great poverty.

Pain also strips away the other things in our lives that we depend on instead of God. When the Russian dissident, Alexander Solzhenitsyn sat in prison, he said, "Bless you prison, bless you, for being in my life, for there, lying on the rotting prison floor, I came to realize that the object of life is not prosperity, as we were made to believe, but the maturing of the human soul."[3]

Sometimes, it is not our pain but the pain of others that propels us to call on God. When the Israelites, just freed from captivity in Egypt, made a golden calf to worship, God was angry and wanted to destroy them. But Moses fasted and prayed for forty days and forty nights on behalf of his people (Deuteronomy 9:18-20). Imagine praying for clients, or anybody, for forty days without ceasing! Moses' love and his concern for his people led him deeper into the ministry of prayer.

Perhaps, the draw to become a praying person is a praying dad, mom, or mentor. The aroma of a praying person is often more inviting than any lesson or sermon on the subject. You won't ever meet Barbara Schultz or Gordon Bracker. They are now spending time with Jesus face to face and loving every minute of it! But their thumbprints are all over the pages of this book. They were not famous people. They were humble folks who loved conversing with God, and their love for God was contagious.

Perhaps you are a librophiliac (book lover!), and it is the pages of history, recording the lives of George Müller, Corrie Ten Boom, Hudson Taylor, or other great prayer notables of history that sparked your hunger to know Him more.

Sometimes we step out on the road of prayer irrespective of pain, concern for others, or following in the footsteps of our mentors. The reasons we start the journey may be less concrete and more internal. Sometimes we simply become aware, like George Müller, that our every breath depends on the One who controls the winds and the waves. We get a glimpse of our smallness and His bigness. We are startled, fascinated and awed by the comparison; and it can draw us to seek Him.

For others, the precious catalyst beckoning them to pray is a heart bursting with thanks for what God has given them.

> We come so often to God, if we come at all, as beggars. We ask and beg: Give me, bless me; help me; guide me; grant me. And that's one necessary level of our existence. But in thanksgiving and adoration we come to God not to ask but to give...We feel not distant from God but close to God. We are like the traveler who is home again at last, the prodigal at a banquet. Those moments may be seldom, but when they happen we know that we were created for God...We know that with certainty in those precious moments when we sing the doxology with so much

inner strength and conviction that we become the
choir directors of the universe.[4]

There is a moment when we first grasp the magnitude of a life
laid down for our own; for a sacrifice made not out of necessity, but
out of love. For many this realization is the first step in a journey of
prayer. It is the kind of realization described by R. C. Sproul as he tells
the story of Wayne Alderson, who experienced a friend's action that
illustrates eloquently what Christ has done for us.

"Scouts out" came the order. Wayne Alderson and "Red" Preston
inched cautiously toward the Siegfried Line as the Allies prepared to
invade Germany in 1945. Within the hour both found themselves in a
trench facing the enemy. A hand grenade tossed at Alderson's feet exploded
and a piece of shrapnel lodged itself in his forehead. Red jumped to shield
his buddy, placing himself between Wayne and the enemy fire. At that
moment Red took the bullet meant for Wayne, and communicated "the
deepest and purest kind of love one man can have for another."[5]

Nearly thirty years later, when Alderson returned to Europe, he
went to Red's gravesite to pay his respects to the man who died so
that he might live.

Jesus Christ took the consequences of sin that were aimed at us.
When we begin to grasp fully His loving sacrifice for us, we gladly
run into the presence of the One who died so that we might live.
We didn't deserve His act of kindness. All our good deeds can never
repay, but only say "Thank you" for His love for us. We, then, can say,
with the former murderer, Paul, "The love of Christ compels us …"
(2 Corinthians 5:14). Ultimately, the strongest magnetic draw upon
the heart of a Christian to become close with God and to rely on His
power is the undeserved kindness He showers upon us.

Starting on the Journey of Prayer

Pain, sorrow, and praying mentors can be the first spark that
ignites in us a desire to launch the journey of prayer. If you have come

to that point and have had that spark ignited, then you are poised to begin. But where do we place our feet? How do we start on this journey that we wish for?

The best way to begin deepening our walk with God is to tell Him that we want to. Just ask Him to increase your hunger for Him. Ask Him to create hunger in your heart for His Word. Ask Him to bring people into your life who will keep nudging you toward Him. Ask Him to help you become a person who nudges others toward Him. God longs to give us such gifts as these (Luke 11:9).

When we ask God for help, we learn humility. Humility teaches us to ask others for help when we are in need. Our journey of prayer is richer and smoother when we walk it with others. Ask some of the godly, mature, praying people in your church to pray for you on the days you counsel individuals. Without sharing the names or issues, ask your colleague, secretary, or administrative assistant to spend a lunch hour praying for the hurting and hurtful people you work with. Start with one other person and pray for more to join you in prayer. After all, asking is where the rebuilding process starts as explained by Charles Spurgeon.

> Whether we like it or not, asking is the rule of the kingdom. "Ask and you shall receive" (John 16: 24). It is a rule that never will be altered in anybody's case. Our Lord Jesus Christ is the elder brother of the family, but God has not relaxed the rule even for Him … If the royal and divine Son of God cannot be exempted from the rule of asking that He may have, you and I cannot expect the rule to be relaxed in our favor.[6]

God will use whatever it takes to draw us to Him, including pain, praise, and praying people. He wants to ignite something new among Christian caregivers. He wants to rebuild the awareness among Christian caregivers about where our help comes from. As long as we caregivers are trying to heal people according to our own wisdom and strength without calling on God's help, we will continue to find the streets of our profession filled with rubble. And He is earnestly looking for those who will be part of the reconstruction project. His loving Father-eyes are relentlessly scanning the horizon to catch a glimpse of us, returning from the far country. He has the celebration banquet already planned when we confess to Him that we have wronged Him by not coming to Him (Luke 15:11-32).

There is one more prayer leader we want to tell you about. He, too, was called to a rebuilding, a restoration of what was lost. Through him God rekindled the desire to repair the brokenness in the land and hearts of the people of Israel.

Let Him Send Me

During one of the many dismal times in Israel's history, God raised up a praying leader. His work began in a king's palace far from his native Jerusalem. Nehemiah was a Jew whose nation was suffering exile—God's judgment because they had worshipped other gods. The Jews had been conquered and scattered, and many were forced to live far from their home.

Nehemiah was serving in the esteemed position of cupbearer to King Artaxerxes (Nehemiah 1:11). He sampled the food and wine prepared for the king before it touched the king's lips. But while Nehemiah served in this place of enormous responsibility, his thoughts were elsewhere. His brother, Hanani, and several others paid him a visit and gave him a heartrending report about his beloved Jerusalem. "Those who survived the exile and are back in the province are in great trouble and disgrace. The wall of Jerusalem is broken down, and its gates have been burned with fire" (Nehemiah 1:3). To the modern reader, broken-down walls might sound trivial, but walls provided ancient cities with protection and security. Without walls, cities invited enemy attack, like a jewelry store with no glass in the window or a city apartment with no door in the doorframe.

This tragic news of his hometown moved Nehemiah to weep, mourn, and pray. The remnant of Israel, the few who had returned from their exile, were in shambles. They were not hopeful and recovering, but desolate and disgraced. Nehemiah wrote, "For some days I mourned and fasted and prayed before the God of heaven" (1:4). He became so consumed with sorrow and seeking God, he stopped eating. He saw God's great reputation being dishonored by the catastrophic conditions in Jerusalem, and the tragic news thrust Nehemiah's face toward God.

Often when we pray God seems to be in no hurry to answer. Nehemiah carried his burden around for four months. One day the king inquired about his cupbearer's unhappy face as he was pouring wine. The question was frightening, since visible sorrow in the king's presence could bring punishment or death. So what did Nehemiah do? He silently prayed to God and then responded honestly to the king about the people's disgrace and his own sorrow over it. God spoke then to Nehemiah in answer to his heartfelt prayers, through the words of the king: "The king said to me, 'What is it you want?'" (2:4).

What is it you want? God had heard him, and was prepared to give him what he wished. He had seen the desires of Nehemiah's heart, and He knew that Nehemiah mourned for his people, and for their disgrace, and for their fall from favor with the Lord and for the dishonor of God's name because the city was in ruins.

Nehemiah responded,

> Then I prayed to the God of heaven, and I answered the king, "If it pleases the king and if your servant has found favor in his sight, let him send me to the city in Judah where my fathers are buried so that I can rebuild it."... And because the gracious hand of my God was upon me, the king granted my requests. (2:4-5, 8)

Not only did the king let Nehemiah go, but upon his request, Artaxerxes also provided timber from the king's forest and safe passage through the bordering nations. And without being asked, the king sent a military escort, to boot (2:9)! Think of it for a moment. A palace waiter gets a leave of absence, building materials, a passport, and military escort, all because he asked God!

The cry of Nehemiah's heart, and the cry of our hearts as caregivers, is for God to use us. He has sent us to broken people, to point them to Him who heals, renews, and rebuilds what has been destroyed.

A Call to Rebuild

When Nehemiah arrived in Jerusalem he took stock of the condition of the walls, and saw that everything his brother had told him was true. He picked his way through rubble and ashes, the remains of the once-beautiful city. But the time for mourning was over. Nehemiah called the demoralized inhabitants to action. "You see the trouble we are in: Jerusalem lies in ruins, and its gates have been burned with fire," he said. "Come, let us rebuild the wall of Jerusalem, and we will no longer be in disgrace." He told them how God had already begun the work: "I also told them about the gracious hand of my God upon me and what the king had said to me" (2:17-18).

And the people responded. From their rubble and disgrace, which they had been unable to repair by themselves, they heard the rallying cry of hope that Nehemiah brought, and "They replied, 'Let us start rebuilding.' So they began this good work" (2:18)!

A renewal of hope and excitement in the whole nation was sparked by this man on whom God's hand rested. They had been broken and cast out, but God had not forgotten them. They had been conquered, but one broken leader turned to God and led all the people to trust God again.

Strengthen My Hands

The people took hope, and the work began. It was not without difficulty. There was much to be done, and the people labored day and night to build and defend the wall. But the tide had been turned and their vision had been restored, and "the people worked with all their heart" (4:6).

Israel's enemies mounted immediate opposition, hating God and His people. Threats, false accusations and violence pummeled Nehemiah and his colaborers. "They were all trying to frighten us," Nehemiah reported, "thinking, 'Their hands will get too weak for the work, and it will not be completed.' But I prayed, 'Now strengthen my hands'" (6:9).

Trusting in God, the people had to defend the progress they had made, fighting to keep their enemies from tearing it all down again. To combat the threat of further invasion, Nehemiah recounted:

> Therefore I stationed some of the people behind the lowest points of the wall at the exposed places, posting them by families, with their swords, spears and bows. After I looked things over, I stood up and said to the nobles, the officials and the rest of the people "Don't be afraid of them. Remember the Lord, who is great and awesome, and fight for your brothers, your sons and your daughters, your wives and your homes." (4:13-14)

Nehemiah continued the work, praying for the strength he needed to withstand opposition and fear, believing in God who had called him to rebuild the walls. And in less than two months, the formidable task, which many had believed impossible, was completed: "So the wall was completed on the twenty-fifth of Elul, in fifty-two days. When all our enemies heard about this, all the surrounding nations were afraid and lost their self-confidence, because they realized that this work had been done with the help of our God" (6:15-16).

Sacred to the Lord

The wall had been rebuilt, the enemies of God's people silenced; but the last piece of Israel's redemption was yet to come. They had long been in exile in foreign nations that did not worship God, far from the life that had made them distinct as God's people. Chapters seven and eight report the discovery and reading of God's Word. When the people heard God's Word, they turned from their sins with great remorse and God brought renewal.

God was changing the hearts of people. The people of Israel had needed the protection of walls around their city. But what they needed most was not walls. It was the peace and security of a restored relationship with God.

The Sound of Rejoicing

Nehemiah's call to rebuild the walls of Jerusalem is similar to the way we feel as we close this book. We echo the call of Nehemiah: Caregivers arise and turn to God for the help we need.

That is our mission as caregivers: to come to the aid of the people; to pray and be sent, and to rebuild what sin has broken. Picture what could happen if the host of well-trained Christian caregivers would begin to pray, to cry out to God to cleanse us and fill us with His Spirit! When Nehemiah prayed, the whole nation followed and began to call upon God. The walls of Jerusalem were rebuilt and there was national renewal and great rejoicing as the people of Israel turned their hearts and lives back to God. When Christian caregivers pray, hurting people will turn to God with them.

When We Part Ways on the Journey of Prayer

And now, dear friends, we have come to the end of our road together. Let's put those in our care in God's hands and trust Him to protect and change them. Our greatest joy would be to know that you have embarked on the journey of prayer, for yourself, and for the people you counsel.

Describing a series of events in her life, author and speaker Jill Briscoe provides a vivid picture of what caregiving is meant to be.

It was a long time ago, when my children were all teenagers. The dating years were upon us, and I lived in a permanent state of internal panic. Fortunately I had a husband who reveled in those years, and so I leaned on him. One day, however, he was away, so I couldn't "lean," and a young man asked my young daughter, Judy, to the school dance. I panicked, until she explained I could come and chaperone. At that I gladly gave permission and the invitation was accepted. Then I looked in my appointment book. Both my husband and I had meetings out of town on the day of the dance. Neither of us could chaperone! I panicked. Suddenly this perfectly nice young man took on another image in my imagination.

I couldn't get out of my commitment, and so I arrived at the meeting in total spiritual disarray. Looking at the program, I saw that there was a prayer room. I made a beeline for it and met Margaret, whose ministry it was to help people like me! I explained my problem, and she listened to me patiently and gave me some Scripture. Then she said I would need to let my daughter go. "After all," she said, "Moses' mother put Moses in the little ark and let him go among the crocodiles." Now that I didn't want to hear. Suddenly all the nice boys that Judy knew took on the shape of crocodiles! Then Margaret told me she would be like Miriam for me. She would stand watch on the riverbank in prayer. In essence, Margaret said to me, "Give me your child." And from that day to this she has carried my child to the upper room and prayed for her. A few months after this incident, I received a package through the mail. It contained a little crocodile with its mouth tied up. "That's what prayer does," said the card![7]

Dream with us for a moment or two: see multitudes of Christian caregivers standing watch among the reeds like Miriam, praying for the people we walk with! There is no end to the legacy a praying caregiver can have on a soul. Picture the results if helping people would begin to pray. Imagine what praying caregivers, supported by a strong team of praying friends, could do on behalf of the hurting and hurtful people we encounter! What might be the results in the transformation of those lives through intimacy in His presence!

We close with this prayer for you on the front lines of the battle.

> May the God of peace, who through the blood
> of the eternal covenant brought back from the dead
> our Lord Jesus, that great Shepherd of the sheep,
> equip you with everything good for doing His will,
> and may He work in us what is pleasing to Him,
> through Jesus Christ, to whom be glory for ever and
> ever. Amen. (Hebrews 13: 20-21)

Reflection

Are you willing to pray that God would transform you to be like Miriam, standing on the riverbank in prayer or like Nehemiah, influencing a nation to change through prayer? Imagine the impact with the people you seek to help!

Notes

[1] Steer, R. *George Müller: Delighted in God* (Bromley, Kent: STL Books), 1975, p. 19.

[2] Cymbala, Jim. *Fresh Wind, Fresh Fire* (Grand Rapids: Zondervan), 1997, p. 19.

[3] Colson, Charles. *The 25th Anniversary: The Conversion of Charles W. Colson* (Washington, DC: BreakPoint), August 1998.

[4] Postema, D. *Space for God* (Grand Rapids: CRC Publications), 1983, pp. 179-180.

[5] Sproul, R. C. *Stronger than Steel* (San Francisco: Harper and Row), 1980, pp. 17-20.

[6] Bounds, E. M. *E. M. Bounds on Prayer* (New Kensington, PA: Whitaker House), 1997, p. 44.

[7] Briscoe, Jill. *Prayer that Works* (Wheaton, IL: Tyndale House Publishers), 2000, p. 52.